How to use this book for your best advantage.

In the first section of the book, look for the answers to these provocative questions ...

• What • When • Where • Why • Which & • How

to use each type of Sulky Thread to achieve professional-looking results in all of your quilting and other creative projects.

We have included general instructions on quilting along with an update on supplies, equipment and such, to make quilting as easy and stimulating as possible.

In the largest section, look for exciting, stimulating, creative Projects & Tips which feature individual and combined uses of Sulky Threads, Sulky Stabilizers, Sulky Puffy Foam and Sulky KK-2000 in quilted projects.

In the last section, you will find Instructions for Finishing and Sources for hard-to-find patterns, notions, etc., used in the projects.

Plus a Bonus!
Pull-out Pattern Sheet

Introduction to the Sulky® Secrets to Successful Quilting with Sulky Threads!

by Joyce Drexler

• What Sulky Threads can we Quilt with?

To those who have never used Sulky Threads either by hand, for machine-fed or free-motion quilting, they are a beautiful discovery that makes quilting even more enjoyable and creative. Virtually all Sulky Threads make the vibrant end result of any of our creative quilting projects exactly what we envisioned when we conceived them.

• When should we use Sulky Threads for Quilting?

The family of Sulky Threads help you add your extra special touch to virtually any type of quilting . . . Hand, Machine and Free-Motion.

• Where should we use Sulky Threads for Quilting?

For "stitching in the ditch" and "invisible applique" quilts, quilters prefer Sulky Polyester Invisible Thread over every other invisible thread because it is made of polyester instead of nylon which gives it a more flexible, soft touch, and makes it more tolerant to the heat of an iron.

Use Sulky 35 wt. Ultra Twist anywhere that you want to create unbelievable tone, texture and dimension.

The rest of the Sulky Decorative thread line should be used wherever and whenever you want your quilting and applique stitching to be beautifully visible with unique color interest. Hand and Machine Quilters love the extraordinarily smooth finish on the Sulky Rayon, Polyester and Metallic Threads which allows them to glide easily through "quilt sandwiches"; because of the ease of using Sulky Rayon, it is becoming a favorite of professional long-arm quilters.

The brilliance of Sulky "Sliver" Metallic is wonderful for adding pizazz to any quilting project. For instance, many quilters who love making "watercolor" quilts find the Sulky Sliver Opalescent #8040 ideal, since it beautifully reflects the color of whatever fabric it crosses.

For those of us who love the country fabric lines of M & M Fabrics by Debbie Mumm and RJR's Thimbleberries fabric line, Sulky has 30 wt. & 40 wt. multi-color threads (#2207, #2208 & #2210) that match perfectly!

Now, there are also Sulky multi-color threads (#2204 & #2205) for jewel tones like the Cherrywood Hand Dyed Fabrics. Of course, Sulky's heavier 30 wt. Rayon is also perfect for Japanese Sashiko Quilting and Primitive Hand-Outline Quilting.

Meet the Author and read on to learn the quilting secrets . . .

Joyce Drexler

Machine Artist, Quilter, Author, Designer, and Co-Managing Partner of Sulky of America, as well as Co-Owner of Speed Stitch, Inc. from Port Charlotte, FL

Joyce and her "Brighty" have found comfort in the quilts she has made over the last 18 years. Joyce is widely recognized as a leader in the field of "Machine Arts and Crafts". Since 1979 she has taught several thousand Retailers and Teachers in Instructor Training Workshops across America and Canada.

Her books have sold well over 400,000 copies and are being sold internationally. She is the producer and co-author of the popular Sulky Book Series "Concepts in Sulky" and "Sulky Secrets to Successful Stabilizing".

Joyce has been published in numerous magazines, and she appears regularly on the PBS TV Programs: Sew Creative; America Sews with Sue Hausmann; Creative Living; Sew Perfect; Quilting From the Heartland; Kaye's Quilting Friends and Martha's Sewing Room. She designed a one-of-a-kind garment for the prestigious Fairfield Fashion Show.

She creates the projects for "Sew Exciting Seminars" and collaborates with Patsy Shields to teach the Sulky Educators that travel nationally conducting these Seminars. She also coordinates the Annual Sulky Challenge.

In 1999, Joyce received the prestigious "Schmetz Golden Needle Award" in acknowledgement of her significant contributions toward enhancing the future of the sewing industry.

• Why do we want to use Sulky Threads for Quilting?

There are over 380 colors of soft, warm, natural-looking Sulky Rayon Threads available, so it is easy to choose just the right solid color, variegated shade, multi-color or Ultra Twist thread for any quilt project.

Quilters interested in extending the longevity of their quilts acknowledge that rayon lasts longer than cotton. Of course, quilts should always be cared for carefully to make them last as long as possible.

On the other hand, quilts that are used daily will also last longer when stitched with Sulky Rayon and Polyester threads rather than cotton and nylon. Sulky Poly Deco is a Polyester Decorative Thread that is colorfast even when using detergents with optical brighteners or bleach. So, if you are making a baby quilt or toddler quilt, or even one for teenagers and college-age kids, using Sulky Poly Deco for quilting will still give you the shine close to Rayon plus the added durability of Polyester.

• Why use Sulky Threads in particular?

Sulky Threads are carefully and thoughtfully engineered to enhance every creative project while working easily in even the most difficult stitching situations. They are made of the highest quality materials, and quality is extremely important since inexpensive, poor quality threads can give you disastrous results.

• How do we use Sulky Threads?

This is what you will learn in this book from the numerous, diversified, creative projects and tips. We will be discussing practical applications and guidelines for decorative thread usage.

Use this book as a source of inspiration, reference and information. If you have more ideas that we haven't touched on, we would love to hear from you. Maybe your tip or idea can be included in our next book.

Write, Fax or E-Mail us:
SULKY OF AMERICA CONSUMER RELATIONS
3113 Broadpoint Dr., Dept. QB
Harbor Heights, FL 33983

FAX: 941-743-4634
E-mail:
info@sulky.com
Visit our **website:**
www.sulky.com
for Free projects and answers to frequently asked questions.

A Beginner's Quick Reference Guide to using SULKY® Threads for Quilting by Machine or Free-Motion

Type of Sulky Thread	Solid Colors available	Variegated Colors available	Multi-Colors available	Type and Size Needle to use	Spool Pin vertical	Spool Pin horizontal	Top Tension	Stitch Length	Can be used in Bobbin	Yardage on Regular Spool	Yardage on King Size Spool
30 wt. Rayon	102	36	18	Quilting or Top Stitch 90/100	ok	ok	Loosen Slightly	2.7 to 3.0	yes	180	500
40 wt. Rayon	283	36	18	Quilting 75/90	ok	ok	Loosen Slightly	2.7 to 3.0	yes	250	850
35 wt. Rayon UltraTwist™	50	0	0	Quilting or Topstitch 90	ok	ok	Loosen Slightly	2.7 to 3.0	yes	200	700
40 wt. Poly Deco™	138	0	0	Quilting 75/90	ok	ok	Loosen Slightly	2.7 to 3.0	yes	250	900
Original Metallic	27	0	9	Metallic 90 or Topstitch 90	ok	ok	Loosen a lot	2.5 to 3.0	yes with care	165 except multi-colors	1000
Sliver™ Metallic	22	0	2	Metallic 90 or Topstitch 90	must	no	Very Loose	2.5 to 3.0	yes with care	250	N/A
Premium Polyester Invisible	2	0	0	Quilting 75/90	ok	ok	Loosen Slightly	2.5	yes wind slowly	440	2400
Premium Polyester Bobbin	2	0	0	N/A	ok	ok	N/A	N/A	yes	475	1500

*You may still need to alter these recommendations
for your specific sewing machine.*

Sulky 30 wt. "Heavy" Decorative Quilting Threads!

500 yds/450 m

SILKY, SHINY, STRONG, WASHABLE & DRY CLEANABLE

1/3 Thicker than 40 wt., 2/3 Thicker than 50 wt. for greater visibility, depth and unique color interest in Quilting Stitches.

Available in 156 Luscious Colors - 102 solid and 54 Variegated and Multi-Colors on both a 180 yd. and 500 yd. snap spool.

Because all Sulky Rayon Thread is made from the highest quality technical raw goods available in the world, you will not have problems with thread breaking, unraveling or deteriorating as a result of poor quality thread. Over 50 years of engineering and research have gone into perfecting the performance of today's Sulky Rayon Threads. From raw goods to twisting, and from dyeing to finishing, all ingredients of thread manufacturing are combined perfectly to produce the shiny, smooth Sulky Thread that is still strong enough to survive today's machine evolution.

Top quality Sulky Threads on King Size Spools are the most sought-after large spool in the market today because they eliminate all of the problems of thread wound on cardboard cores or mini-cones:

*   *No more thread falling off the spool and tangling under the spool pin.*
*   *No more unprotected, exposed thread at the end of the spool or cone that can become trapped by the spool holder.*
*   *No more need to use thread nets.*
*   *No more tangled messes in your thread storage boxes with Sulky's snap-spools.*
*   *No more spools or cones that don't turn smoothly and evenly on vertical spool pins.*

The Cross Roads Variation Block **features the look of** *Hand Quilting Stitches but it is done by Machine* **using Sulky 30 wt. Variegated Rayon #2124**

4

Sulky 40 wt. "Light but Strong" Decorative Quilting Threads!

Sulky 40 wt. Rayon is a man-made fiber that has very much the same luster of silk and silk's smoothness, but is stronger than both silk and cotton thread, and therefore is perfect for quilting.

Available in 337 Vibrant Colors - 283 Solid Colors and 54 Variegated and Multi-Colors on both a 250 yd. and 850 yd. Snap Spool.

Snap-Open Spools
for easy storage of thread ends.
Sulky 40 wt. is perfect for:
Sewing Machines, Embroidery
Machines, and Sergers.

- Because of Sulky's silky finish and legendary quality, it will smoothly glide through a quilt top, batting and backing when stitched either by hand or machine.
- Quilting with Sulky Rayon Thread will give you the soft, warm, natural look and long-lasting results that you desire.
- Sulky Rayon does <u>not</u> fray and fuzz in the machine, and it does <u>not</u> shrink like cotton.
- Sulky Rayon is cross-wound on the small spool to ensure easier thread flow on any machine, and consistently superior stitch quality.
- Sulky has color numbers and weight sizes printed on each small spool for easy identification.

- Sulky Rayon is completely Machine Washable in either hot or cold water. Use a laundry soap or detergent that does <u>not</u> contain chlorine or optical brighteners.
- Sulky Rayon is Dry Cleanable.

If you love to do machine embroidery, you should know that the vast majority of embroidery designs are digitized for 40 wt. Rayon. Because of its excellent runability, unparalleled quality, and huge selection of colors, Sulky is the first choice of home embroiderers. Sulky 40 wt. Rayon is also easier to use than polyester because it has less stretch and stretch memory. Sulky Rayon lays down nicely in the design without the occasional thread pull-ups which occur when using polyester. Sulky 40 wt. Rayon's look is more soft, warm and natural compared to the almost "plasticky" look of polyester. Because of polyester's added, unnecessary strength, it causes the acceleration of wear on the machine's moving parts and in the bobbin and needle thread path.

The Rail Fence Block features the Feather Stitch, a decorative machine stitch using Sulky 40 wt. Multi-Color Rayon #2247

5

Sulky Decorative 40 wt. Poly Deco™ & Sulky Premium Polyester Invisible Quilting Threads!

Sulky 40 wt. Poly Deco is a top quality, strong, 100% polyester, shiny thread that is especially suited for children's clothing, work clothes, sport clothes, and any garment that will need to be washed frequently. Poly Deco can be laundered with soap containing optical brighteners and bleach. Since Poly Deco has more stretch and stretch memory than Rayon, the top tension generally has to be reduced, and the type and amount of stabilizer(s) can be different than when using Rayon.

Sulky Premium Polyester Invisible Thread:
- Perfect for machine "hand-look" quilting, stitching in the ditch, and invisible applique. Ideal for hems.
- Very fine .004 monofilament that is soft enough for baby quilts or garments that will be worn next to the skin.
- Wonderful to use as a lightweight bobbin thread for decorative stitches and embroidery. Compatible with both Sulky Metallics and Rayons.
- Available in both smoke for darker fabrics and clear for lighter fabrics.
- Has no rough edges on the spool to tangle, snarl, or break the thread.
- Spool turns easily on vertical spool pins without thread spilling off.
- Thread flows easily off horizontal spool pins.

Because it is 100% polyester, it does not melt with normal ironing through the cotton setting.

The *Log Cabin Block* (above) features the quilting look of a *Decorative Leaf Stitch Pattern by Machine* following a scalloped design using Sulky Poly Deco all-purpose Thread #1255.

The *Nine Patch Block* (right) features Sulky Premium Smoke Invisible Thread *Stitched in the Ditch* to stabilize the block. Then Sulky 30 wt. Rayon Thread #1208 was stitched *"free-motion"* over a Sulky Solvy Swirl Pattern. A *Look of Hand Quilting but by Machine* was achieved by using Sulky 30 wt. Rayon #1192 in the bobbin and Smoke Invisible in the needle with the top tension tightened to the maximum to bring up the bobbin thread.

6

Sulky Decorative Original & Sliver™ Metallic Quilting Threads!

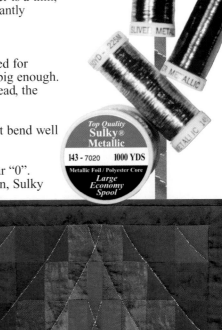

Sulky Sliver Metallic Thread comes in 24 brilliant solid and multi-colors. Sliver is a thin, flat, ribbonlike polyester film that is metalized with aluminum to make it brilliantly reflective.

Hints for success when using Sliver:
- Use a 14/90 sewing, topstitch, or embroidery needle. Needles that are labeled for "metallic threads" still need to be 14/90 for Sliver. The 12/80's are just not big enough.
- It is important to use Sliver on a vertical spool pin. Since Sliver is a flat thread, the twisting action from a horizontal spool pin can cause breakage.
- Sew slower.
- All Metallics hate abrasion and small stitches because Metallics simply don't bend well into small stitches.
- Use a soft, pliable Sulky Stabilizer to properly stabilize your fabric.
- Lower your top tension substantially. On some machines this may mean near "0".
- Use a lightweight Sulky thread in the bobbin, either a matching 40 wt. Rayon, Sulky Bobbin or Polyester Invisible Thread.
- Dry clean or Machine wash in cool or warm water, dry at low heat setting; cover with a press cloth to iron.

Sulky Original Metallic Thread is available in 36 solid and multi-colors that are made by wrapping the finest metallic foil around a strong polyester core to produce a soft, smooth thread that easily glides through your quilting projects.

Hints for success with Metallic Threads:
- Use a 14/90 sewing, topstitch, or embroidery needle. Needles that are labeled for "metallic threads" still should be 14/90's.
- Reduce top tension.
- Sew slower.
- Stabilize properly.
- Use a lightweight Sulky Bobbin Thread.
- Dry clean or wash in cool or warm water. Avoid chlorine bleach or other optical brighteners. Iron on low temperature.

The *Bargello Block* (above) features *Straight Stitch Quilting* at a 3.0 length using Sliver Metallic Quilting Thread #8024.

TIP: *If breakage still occurs, a thread lubricant, such as Tri-Flow™, Sewers Aid™, or a spray silicone, approved for use on your sewing machine may help to ease the thread through rough or tight spots in the thread path. Check with your sewing machine dealer before using any lubricant on your machine.*

The *Sulky Spinning Star Block* (left) was first *Stitched in the Ditch* to stabilize it. It features *"free-motion" Meandering Quilting* and a Sulky Solvy Swirl Pattern using Sulky Original Metallic Decorative Quilting Thread #7022. (Swirl Design located on page 72.)

7

Sulky Ultra Twist™

Because each of the 50 Sulky Ultra Twist shades is made by twisting together two existing Sulky solid colored strands, you can stitch Ultra Twist individually or use it to accent, highlight, or blend with either or both solid colors to create unbelievable tone, texture and dimension in your quilted projects. (The two solid color numbers are printed on the end of the spool.)

Each color family has several shades of Ultra Twist so you can create different, dramatic shading effects within the same project. Great for applique, free motion embroidery and quilting.

Premium Sulky® ULTRA TWIST
700 yds/640 m
SILKY, SHINY, STRONG, WASHABLE & DRY CLEANABLE

Ultra Twist Sulky Rayon

Regular 40 wt. Sulky Rayon

The *Hole in the Barn Door Block* (left) features the look of *Echo Quilting* by machine using Sulky Ultra Twist #3006 Quilting Thread.

The *Foundation Piecing House Block* (right) features the look of *Decorative Built-in Stitches for Quilting* and embellishing using Sulky Ultra Twist #3003, #3006, #3030 & #3013, and Sliver Metallic #8033 & #8020 Threads.

8

Combine Sulky Threads for some spectacular Quilted Effects!

The *Kansas Troubles Block (above)* features the look of EZ Quilting by Wrights *Stitch-Thru™ Tear-Away Stencils* Pattern "Dahlia Dandy". Quilted by machine using Sulky 30 wt. Rayon #1192 and Sulky Metallic #7029 through one Quilting or Embroidery Needle, Size 14/90.

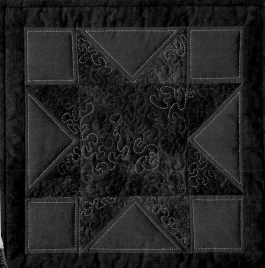

The *Tail of Benjamin's Kite Block* (above) features the look of Sulky Metallic #7016 and Sulky Sliver Metallic #8003 together through one Quilting or Embroidery Needle, Size 14/90 and stitched in the ditch.

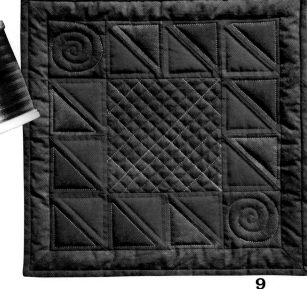

The *Sulky Simple Star Block (above)* features the look of the *Stipple Quilting Stitch* in two different sizes using Sulky 30 wt. Variegated Thread #2131 and Sulky 30 wt. #1045 for *Echo Quilting.*

The *Double "X" Variation Block (right)* features the look of *Echo Quilting* using Sulky 30 wt. Rayon #1045 Thread at a 3.0 straight stitch setting and *Cross Hatch Quilting* which looks like several colors of thread must have been used, but only Sulky 30 wt. Multi-Color Thread #2204 was actually used. The Swirl Design was stitched over a Sulky Solvy Pattern. (Swirl Design located on page 72.)

9

Please read these tips before you begin any project.

IF YOU PRE-WASH YOUR FABRICS -

Be sure to press and spray with Magic Sizing™ to make them easier to handle. Pre-washing is a great idea for the hand-dyed Cherrywood Fabrics to remove any excess dye that might remain.

CUTTING -

Treat yourself to a new blade in your rotary cutter. Having a good cut will reflect in the accuracy of your overall construction. When beginning to cut using your rotary cutter, mat and quilter's ruler, first make a slight cut backwards at the beginning of the cut. Having your pinkie off the ruler and on the table (opposite cutting edge) will help stabilize the ruler. Stagger strips when cutting multiple layers. Square them up with the lines on the ruler. Always cut off selvage edges.

SEWING THREAD -

Use cotton, poly/cotton, or a good quality 100% polyester machine sewing thread, off-white or cream for relatively light colored fabrics, gray for medium toned fabrics, and brown for dark fabrics.

By pressing seams to the side, stitching will not show if your machine tension is set correctly, and there will be less stress on the seam thread.

MAKE SURE YOU ARE USING AN ACCURATE 1/4" SEAM ALLOWANCE THROUGHOUT THE PROJECT -

Measure your very first seam to be positive it is exactly 1/4". Especially when making the Sampler Quilt, all the blocks must measure a true 12-1/2" square before they are sewn into the quilt.

Most machines today have an accurate 1/4" foot available either with the machine or as an accessory. With some machines it is possible to use the edge of the presser foot as a 1/4" guide. However, to be sure, stitch some sample seams using scrap fabric, and measure the seam allowance carefully. If you have a computerized machine, there is usually an easy way to set the machine for an exact 1/4" seam by changing the needle position.

USE THE SAME SEWING MACHINE AND FOOT -

To ensure that the seam allowances stay a true and uniform 1/4", use the same machine and foot when piecing the blocks for any quilt.

MATCHING SEAMS -

Use extra-long quilting straight pins or silk pins to help match seams. Simply put the pin point straight through the first layer seam joint, then carefully look to see that the point again penetrates at the second layer seam joint that you are trying to match. Then, when you penetrate the layers the second time, repeat the procedure so that the pin repeats its penetration in the seam line for both layers. It's a snap - and also a sure thing!

SECURING THREADS -

You will **not** need to backstitch at the beginning and ending of pieced strips and squares since these edges will become seam allowances as you continue to cut and piece. However, handle sewn pieces carefully so stitching does not come undone. Since it is always best to lock off your first and last stitch, if you have a relatively new machine, it probably has a single pattern button or a lock stitch button which you can use to lock off your first and last stitch. That does not mean back stitch. Leave tails long and thread them through a hand needle. Bury the threads in between the top and bottom layers of the quilt.

PRESS ALL SEAM ALLOWANCES -

Press all seams to one side toward darkest fabric because seams might show through light-colored fabric when batting and backing are placed behind the face of the quilt.

DO NOT PRESS SEAMS OPEN -

Unless instructed to do so, do not press any seams open. To avoid distorting the fabric shape when pressing seams, press only (*do not slide the iron*). Press the wrong side first, then the right side.
- **No steam**
- **Press first from the back, setting the seam.**
- **Press again from the front.**

MOST-USED MACHINE QUILTING STITCHES -

"Stitching in the Ditch" - This is one of the most basic of quilting stitches by machine. The "ditch" is actually the seam line between pieces, blocks, sashing and borders. Use the hand wheel to manually lower the needle into the seam line. Always tie on or anchor your stitches. Then straight stitch along the lower side of the seam line (the one that doesn't have the seam allowances pressed toward it). When crossing a seam intersection, the seam allowance may shift to the opposite side. Simply follow along whichever side doesn't have the seam allowance. Usually stitched with Sulky Invisible Thread - Clear for light-colored fabrics and smoke for dark fabrics. *Experiment with stitching in the ditch using Sulky Metallic or Sliver Thread. It really gives depth to the block.*

"Crosshatch Stitching" - A grid created by making one set of parallel lines intersect perpendicularly with another set of parallel lines. Use a Quilter's Ruler and rolling chalk marker to draw a diagonal line, usually in the center or from corner to corner of either a block, sashing or border. Use a quilt guide to space the grid, or you can draw it out. Tie on and tie off at the beginning and end of each row of stitching. To better show off your stitching, use a slightly longer stitch length (3.0 or more) and heavier Sulky 30 wt. thread. Consider using decorative stitches, twin-needles and Sulky Variegated and Multi-Colors.

"Stipple (tight); Meandering or Serpentine (loose)" - Set up your machine for "Free-Motion" (see page 55). Use a machine embroidery hoop and/or a darning foot on the machine. Guide the quilt smoothly, making puzzle shapes that are s-shaped curves. Try to keep the stitches looking uniform in stitch length by developing a rhythm between the speed of the machine and movement of the quilt top. Generally, stitching lines will not cross over each other. Stippling lines generally are no more than 1/8" to 1/4" apart, while Meandering is a more loosely spaced stitch.

"Echo Quilting" - A line of stitching that repeats the shape once or in multiples. It can be done "Free-Motion" or machine fed. (See Stippling above and page 55 for free-motion set-up.) If machine fed, use either a clear foot, walking foot or even-feed foot, and a 3.0 straight stitch length; stitch consistently 1/8" or 1/4" away from the seam line of the pieces that make up the blocks or appliqued design. Start your stitching on a smooth edge, not at a point. Always tie on and tie off.

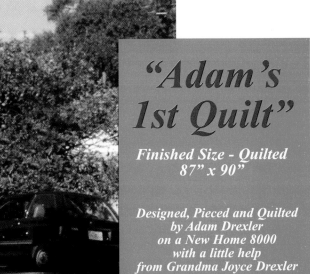

"Adam's 1st Quilt"

Finished Size - Quilted 87" x 90"

Designed, Pieced and Quilted by Adam Drexler on a New Home 8000 with a little help from Grandma Joyce Drexler

As seen on the PBS TV Show - "SEW CREATIVE"

When Adam was 5 years old in 1993, he began sewing on the Computerized New Home 8000 when it first arrived in his Grandpa's Sewing Store. Adam's Dad, Eric Drexler managed the Charlotte County Sewing Center in Port Charlotte, FL and Adam would spend time there on weekends and after school.

In 1994, Eric took Adam to a New Home Dealer Training Meeting and everyone there was amazed that Adam knew how to do embroidery on the machine. When he returned from the meeting he promptly began demonstrating embroidery in the store. He had so much fun showing the instructors in the store, his Grandma, and customers all about the machine.

At age 10, Grandma Joyce Drexler and Adam began getting together whenever they could to work on this quilt. Because of Grandma's traveling schedule and Adam's Baseball, Boy Scouts, Church and School schedule, time together was precious and little. So it took 2 years! Finally, at age 12, Adam appeared with his Grandma on the SEW CREATIVE TV Program and shared his quilt with everyone! The Quilt turned out great, but Grandma says, "The time spent together was the best part."

Adam used a Sulky 30 wt. Multi-Colored Rayon #2204 in both the needle and bobbin. Grandma "stitched in the ditch" (see page 10 for more on "Stitching in the Ditch") of the Sashing with Sulky Smoke Invisible Thread to stabilize the quilt sandwich. Then Adam used a beading stitch to stitch from corner-to-corner on all of the squares in the blocks. You could also elongate your straight stitch to 3.0 for a similar looking stitch. A "feather stitch" was used along the Sashing and Borders.

Fabric Credits: Hoffman Fabrics & Kona Bay

A Perfect Quilt for a Beginner.
✄ Cutting Guide for a Queen Size Quilt

Always cut the selvages off the fabric before cutting strips.

- ✄ 1/2 yd. each of four solid Fabrics cut into 4" x 44" strips
- ✄ 1/2 yd. each of four printed Fabrics cut into 4" x 44" strips
- ✄ 2 yds. - solid black Fabric for Sashing cut into 4" x 44" strips
- ✄ 1 yd. print Fabric for Border cut into 4" x 44" strips
- ✄ 1/3 yd. for each side border (one purple and one blue in our quilt - because we ran out of fabric!)

- ✄ 5/8 yd. - Fabric for Binding
- ✄ 5-1/2 yds. Fabric for Backing
- ✄ Batting - Queen Size

SUPPLIES:
- Zig-Zag Sewing Machine with 1/4" Foot and Even-Feed Foot
- Quality Sewing Thread
- New 14/90 Quilting Needle
- Sulky 30 wt Rayon Multi-Color Thread #2204
- Sulky KK 2000 Temporary Spray Adhesive
- Safety Pins for Basting

2

MAKING STRIP SETS:

1. Use a 1/4" seam to sew **Strip Set "A"** consisting of alternating 4" x 44" solid and printed fabrics. Adam chose his printed strips randomly.

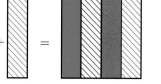

PRESS the seams up for this set. Turn the strip set sideways, then use a rotary cutter, mat and ruler to cut it into 4" strips.

2. Sew **Strip Set "B"** consisting of alternating prints and solid fabrics

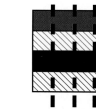

PRESS the seams down for this set. Turn the strip set sideways, then use a rotary cutter, mat and ruler to cut it into 4" strips.

3

Re-sew the cut sets into blocks by combining 3 strips together, alternating the direction of the strip. Match seams as you combine strips - pin them together for accuracy.

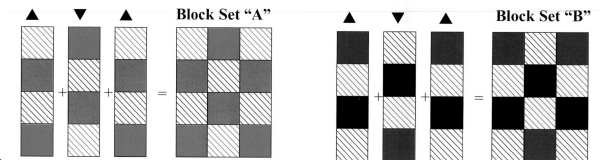

Block Set "A"

Block Set "B"

COMBINE THE BLOCKS WITH SASHING TO MAKE THE QUILT TOP:

1. Measure your Blocks to be sure they are of an equal measurement. Block them if needed (see page 20) to get a uniform size.

2. Cut 20 Sashing Strips 4" x 13". Arrange your Blocks in the desired order.

3. Use a 1/4" seam to sew Sashing between the Blocks.

4. Sew a 4" x 67" horizontal Sashing onto each end and in between each row of Blocks.

5. Add Sashing to each long side.

6. Add print Border to all four sides.

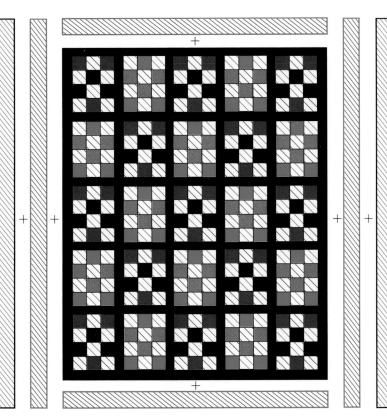

For extra width, add a border strip of a print to each long side as desired. (See page 159 for more information on adding Straight Edge Border Strips.) With the added Border Strips, this quilt will fit a queen-size bed.

PIN BASTE YOUR QUILT:

Refer to page 160 for more information on quick basting a quilt.

1. Use a 1/2" seam allowance to piece together a quilt backing that is at least 4" larger on all sides than the quilt top. **PRESS SEAMS OPEN** and press out all wrinkles.

2. Make a Quilt Sandwich:
   First Layer - Quilt Back - right side down
   Second Layer - Batting
   Third (top) Layer - Quilt Top - right side up

3. Grandpa (Fred Drexler) helped Adam pin baste his quilt together on the ping-pong table so they could spend some quality time together too.

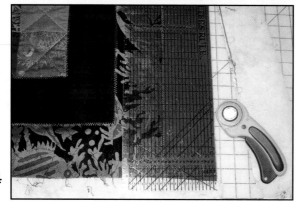

MARK IT:

To make quilting easier, Adam used a Quilter's Ruler and Chalk Rolling Marker to mark a line from corner to corner through the 12 squares that made up each block so he would have a straight line to follow.

QUILT IT:

Refer to page 161 for Tips on Successful Quilting.

Machine Set-up:

- Even Feed Foot
- New Quilting Needle size 14/90
- Thread - Sulky Polyester Smoke Invisible and Sulky 30 wt. #2204
- Beading Stitch or a Straight Stitch at 3.0 length

1. Grandma "stitched in the ditch" using Sulky Smoke Invisible between all the Sashing Strips to stabilize the quilt sandwich.

2. Adam used the Beading Stitch and Sulky 30 wt. #2204 to stitch from corner to corner on all the squares in the blocks.

3. Adam and Grandma stitched in the center of the seams of the Sashing using the "Feather Stitch".

4. Once all the quilting was finished, Adam trimmed off the excess batting and backing.

5. Grandma added the binding and hanging sleeve.

Sulky Cherrywood Sampler Quilt

Designed and Pieced by Joyce Drexler and Patti Lee. Quilted by Evelyn Howard
and Tina Ignatowicz (See the Sulky Garden Twist version on the back cover.)

Piecing Guide for Sulky Sampler Blocks

Machine Set-up for Piecing Blocks:

- Use only high quality sewing thread in the needle and bobbin.

- Universal Needle size 80/85.

- 1/4" Foot, Tape or Seam Guide for making exact quarter-inch seams and/or changing the needle position to make a 1/4" seam so blocks finish true to 12-1/2"square.

- Select Needle-Down Position (if available).

- Straight Stitch Setting.

- Stitch Length 2.0 to 2.5 (12-14 stitches per inch).

General Supplies

- 4-1/2" and 6-1/2" wide Quilter's Ruler

- Cutting Mat or Cut 'n Press Pad

- Large Rotary Cutter

- Small Scissors

- Dry Iron & Ironing Pad

- Size 90 Quilting Machine Needles

- White Sewing Thread for Sulky Garden Twist, or Purple for Cherrywood Jewel Tone Fabric

- 1/4" Foot or Seam Guide

- Half-Square Triangle Paper 1-1/2", 3", 3-1/2" and 4" finished sizes.

Wallhanging or Lap Quilt

Finished Size: 63" x 78"

Each unfinished block is 12-1/2" square. The seam allowance is 1/4" throughout. Each block is finished to 12" square. Yardage figured on 44" wide fabric. (Note: Cherrywood Fabric is not 44" wide.)

Fabrics needed to make the Blocks. See the Fabric Key on facing page.

Color 1 - 1 yd.

Color 2 - 1 yd.

Color 3 - 1 yd.

Color 4 - 1 yd.

Color 5 - 1/2 yd.

Color 6 - 1 yd.

Fabric Needed for Sashing
Color 6 - 1-1/4 yd.

Fabric Needed for Border Accent
Color 3 - 1/2 yd.

Fabric Needed for Border
Color 6 - 1-1/4 yd.

Fabric Needed for
Backing & Sleeve
Color of your choice - 5 yds.

Fabric Needed for Binding
Color 6 - 1/2 yd.

See pull-out pattern sheet for fabric cutting layout for Blocks only.

Make a Fabric Key for your Sampler Quilt

For easy referral, make a Fabric Key for yourself, like we did here, using snips of your fabrics labeled Colors 1-6.

In The Beginning™ Garden Twist Collection

Cherrywood™ Suede-Look Cotton

COLOR 1

White Background with Blue & Pink Roses

Fuchsia (Cherrywood 816 Deep Gems #7)

COLOR 2

White Background with Floral Bouquet Print

Raspberry (Cherrywood 816 Deep Gems #6)

COLOR 3

White Background with Overall Floral

Purple (Cherrywood 234 Eggplant)

COLOR 4

Mottled Light Green

Blue (Cherrywood 296 New Navy)

COLOR 5

Mottled Dark Green

Teal (Cherrywood 840 Indigo to Evergreen #4)

Note: Basically these six exchanges are true, but there are some exceptions in some of the Cherrywood blocks for color harmony.

COLOR 6

Green Batik

Pine (Cherrywood 840 Indigo to Evergreen #6)

Nine Patch

The perfect place to begin.
"Strip Piecing Method".

**The first of 12 Blocks
in the Sampler Quilt.**

Arrange the next set of strips in this order:
Color 4, Color 2 and Color 4 as shown above.

This group will be called Set 2.

1

✂ Cutting Guide
Use the 4-1/2" Ruler

**Always cut the selvages off the fabric
before cutting strips.**

✂ Cut three 4-1/2" x 22" strips - Color 4
✂ Cut three 4-1/2" x 22" strips - Color 2

2

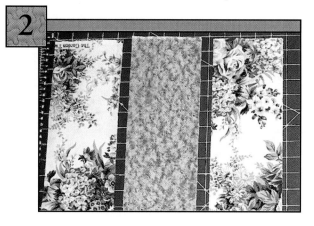

Arrange one set of the strips in this order:
Color 2, Color 4 and Color 2 as shown above.

This group will be called Set 1.

3

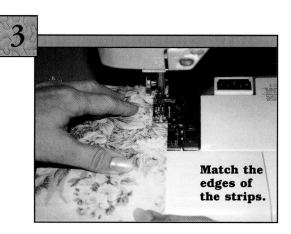

**Match the
edges of
the strips.**

Using Set 1 strips, place right sides of Color
2 and Color 4 together; keep raw edges
together while sewing them.

**Check the accuracy of your first seam. Is it
a perfect 1/4"? If not, now is the time to
make the necessary adjustments. You may
need to change your needle position or
move the seam guide. Do whatever it takes
to obtain that perfect 1/4" throughout the
Sampler Quilt Block construction.**

*Continue sewing Set 1 together, then sew
the Set 2 strips together.*

*Sulky Girl
illustrated by
Natalie Sorenson*

Sulky Sewing Tip

*Use the **NEEDLE-DOWN SETTING** (when available) to keep your place as you reposition your hands while sewing the fabric strips.*

But, before removing the fabric, always make sure the needle is out of the fabric and the take-up lever is at its highest point before pulling fabric toward the left/back side of the machine to clear the top thread from around the hook area so the thread doesn't get jammed in the mechanism. It will also keep your needle from bending and hitting the throat plate of the machine, possibly breaking the needle and/or making a nick in the throat plate that could later cause thread breakage.

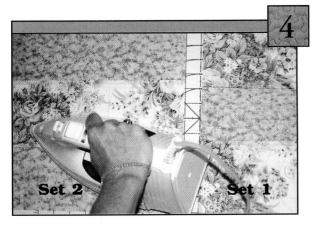

Set 2   Set 1

PRESS the seams toward Color 4 on each Strip Set so the seams will mesh together later when Strip Sets are re-cut and re-sewn to create the Nine Patch.

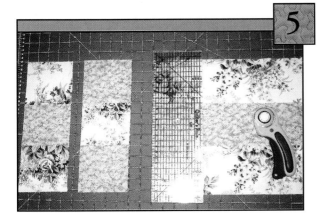

Use the 4-1/2" Ruler to cut Set 1 and Set 2 into 4-1/2" x 12-1/2" strips. Arrange the strips so one strip from Strip Set 1 is on the left, one strip from Strip Set 2 is in the middle and another strip from Strip Set 1 is on the right.

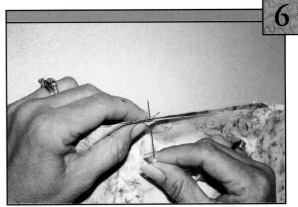

Properly pin to match the squares at seams before stitching rows. Place right sides together and raw edges even. The pin should be in the seam thread on both sides.

To ensure smooth seams with perfect intersections, slow down as you approach each seam. Stop with the needle down, raise the presser foot, and lift the strip slightly from the machine bed. Make certain that seam allowances on the underside are still turned in the direction that they were pressed. Then, lower the presser foot and continue sewing.

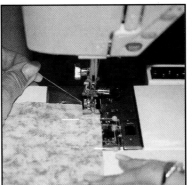

It is important to hold the needle and bobbin threads at the edge when you first begin stitching to keep them from being pulled into the machine causing a thread jam.

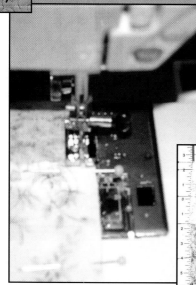

Stitch right up to a pin, but not over it. You may want to use the Even Feed Foot to help in feeding the fabric so seams can be matched perfectly. Many machine quilters can successfully match seams without pinning by nesting the two seams with their fingers. Find which way works best for you.

Press seams toward the center of the block.

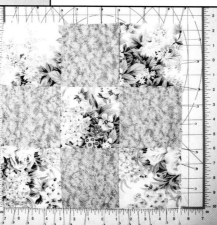

Measure the block to be sure it is exactly 12-1/2" square. If necessary, place your block on a pin board that shows the 12-1/2" square measurement needed. Lightly mist the block and press while easing the block to the correct size. Pin until dry.

Set aside the Nine Patch Block for now.

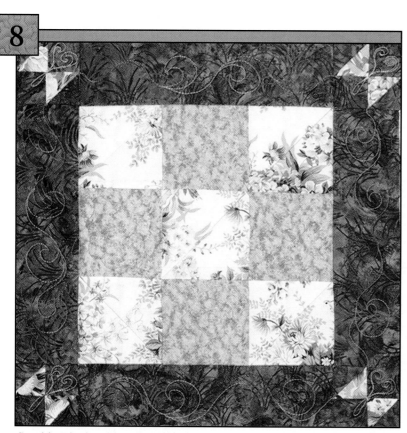

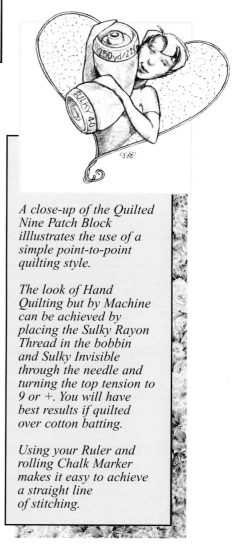

A close-up of the Quilted Nine Patch Block illlustrates the use of a simple point-to-point quilting style.

The look of Hand Quilting but by Machine can be achieved by placing the Sulky Rayon Thread in the bobbin and Sulky Invisible through the needle and turning the top tension to 9 or +. You will have best results if quilted over cotton batting.

Using your Ruler and rolling Chalk Marker makes it easy to achieve a straight line of stitching.

Set this Block aside and quilt it when you have assembled the Sampler Quilt. See pages 69 and 157-160.

Now that you know how to make a NINE PATCH, use the same technique to make a border.

Joyce designed and quilted this one using Sulky 40 wt. Multi-Color Rayon Thread #2245 over Fairfield's Low-Loft Polyester Batting.

The Multi-Color Sulky Rayon is the perfect complement to the gorgeous colors in the M & M Fabrics used in this Autumn Quilt.

21

Log Cabin

An all-time favorite block
"Strip Piecing Method".

Position the **Center Block, Color 3**, so the print is laying in the direction you want when completed (if it's a one way design). Lay **Strip Color 1** right side down on the right-hand side of the 2-1/2" square, matching edges. Stitch them together with a 1/4" seam.

3

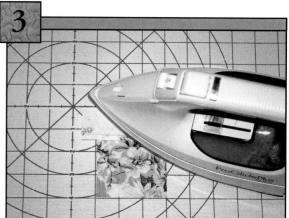

BEGINNERS, PRESS SEAM ALLOWANCE TOWARD THE CENTER BLOCK THROUGHOUT.

Do not slide the iron, lift the iron each time you move it - PRESS ONLY. Always press toward the Center Square to keep the strips from becoming distorted.

1

✂ Cutting Guide
Use the 4-1/2" Ruler

Always cut the selvages off the fabric before cutting strips.

✂ Cut one 1-1/2" x 44" strip - Color 1
✂ Cut one 1-1/2" x 44" strip - Color 2
✂ Cut one 2-1/2" square - Color 3
✂ Cut one 1-1/2" x 44" strip - Color 4
✂ Cut one 1-1/2" x 44" strip - Color 5
✂ Cut one 1-1/2" x 44" strip - Color 6

4

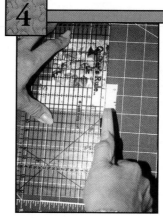

Once **Strip 1** is folded out and pressed, use your ruler, rotary cutter and mat to **trim off Strip 1** flush with the **Center Square** at both ends.

Turn the work one rotation to the left or counter clockwise to add next strip.

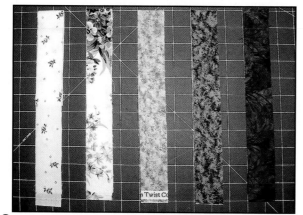

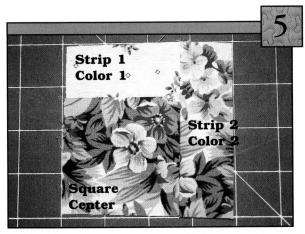

Lay **Strip 2, Color 2,** right side down on the right-hand side of the Center Square and Strip 1; line up the strip with the raw edges of the center square and Strip 1, as shown previously. Stitch an exact 1/4" seam.

Press the seam allowance toward the Center Block. Once the 2nd Strip is pressed, trim **Strip 2** flush with the Square and Strip 1.

Add **Strip 3, Color 4,** in the same manner as Steps 1-4. The bulk of the developing block will always be to the left of the needle. Photo shows Strip 3 trimmed.

Add **Strip 4, Color 5,** in the same manner as Steps 1-4.

Round 2. Go around again. Add **Strip 5, Color 6,** in the same manner as in Steps 1-4. Measure your block at this point. (Block should measure 5-1/2". Make any adjustments now, if needed.) Continue adding Strips Color 1, 2, 4, 5, and 6 until the block is exactly 12-1/2" square as measured with your 12-1/2" Quilter's Square.

Photo shows Strip 5 trimmed.

This photo shows the back of the finished Log Cabin Block so you can see how pressing to the Center Square makes for a perfect finish.

This method of pressing keeps your strips more stable as others are added.

Once you have more experience making Log Cabin Blocks, you may wish to press all the seams to the outside to create less bulk.

◀ **Add Strip 4 Color 5**

"Angels in My Cabin"

Designed by Joyce Drexler, Quilted by Marilyn Badger

You can take any theme fabric and use it as your focal point (center). The size and shape that you cut your center will determine the look of the block, i.e., if it will be a square or a rectangle.

Fabrics:
Alexander Henry's Angel Print; smaller prints are M&M fabrics.

This quilt was quilted by Marilyn Badger on a professional long-arm quilting machine using Sulky Sliver #8007, #8040 and Original Metallic #7027.

Patsy's Oriental Quilt

Designed and
Quilted by
Patsy Shields
using Sulky
Sliver
Metallic #8007
on the front
and Sulky
30 wt. Rayon
Multi-Color #2240
on the back.

Set this Block aside and quilt it when you have assembled the Sampler Quilt. See pages 69 and 157-160.

A close-up of the Quilted Log Cabin Block shows how effective a clam shell design can be. You can use a stencil to mark the quilt block or, if you don't have a stencil available, try a plate or cup to achieve the curve.

25

Using a 1/4" seam allowance, put right sides together and sew strips together in color order from 1 to 6. Press seam allowances toward the darkest fabric (Color 6). Do not slide the iron. Lift the iron each time you move it - PRESS ONLY.

Bargello

Looks complicated --- but it's not!
"Strip Piecing Method".

After pressing, use a 1/4" seam allowance to sew the long side of Color 1 and Color 6 together, making the Strip Set into a circular tube.

✄ Cutting Guide
Use the 6-1/2" Ruler

Always cut the selvages off the fabric before cutting strips.

✄ Cut one 2-1/2" x 22" strip - Color 1
✄ Cut one 2-1/2" x 22" strip - Color 2
✄ Cut one 2-1/2" x 22" strip - Color 3
✄ Cut one 2-1/2" x 22" strip - Color 4
✄ Cut one 2-1/2" x 22" strip - Color 5
✄ Cut one 2-1/2" x 22" strip - Color 6

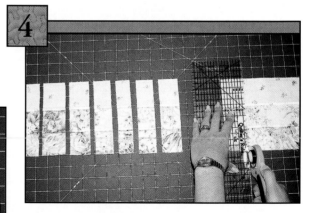

Lay the Strip Set flat with three colors showing. Cut the Strip Set into varied width strips. Start with one that is 2-3/8", the second strip should be 2" then make each following Strip Set 1/4" smaller until you reach the Strip Set 5 which is 1-1/4". Then make each following Strip Set 1/4" larger back up to Strip #8. Cut Strip #9 2-3/8".

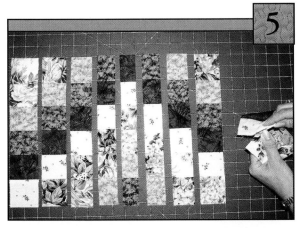

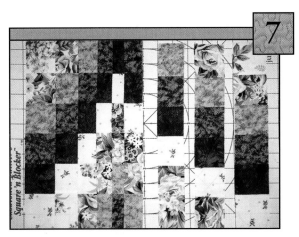

USING A SEAM RIPPER, unsew each Strip Set between colors as follows: between colors 1 & 2 for 2-3/8" strips; between colors 2 & 3 for 2" strips; between colors 3 & 4 for 1-3/4" strips; between colors 4 & 5 for 1-1/2" strips; between colors 5 & 6 for 1-1/4" strip. Lay out Strip Sets to form the Bargello Pattern.

RE-SEW INTO A BLOCK in the following order, being certain to pin seams so they match perfectly:

Strip 1 - 2-3/8"
Strip 2 - 2"
Strip 3 - 1-3/4"
Strip 4 - 1-1/2"
Strip 5 - 1-1/4"
Strip 6 - 1-1/2"
Strip 7 - 1-3/4"
Strip 8 - 2"
Strip 9 - 2-3/8"

Does your block measure 12-1/2"?

If not, "BLOCK IT", as explained in the Nine Patch Block, page 20.

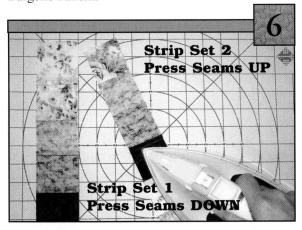

RE-PRESS SEAM ALLOWANCES so every other Strip Set has seam allowances facing opposite directions so they will nest together and lay flat when the Block is sewn.

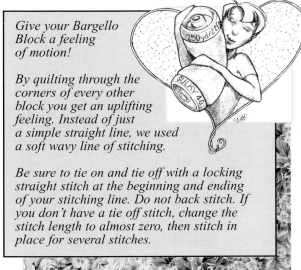

Give your Bargello Block a feeling of motion!

By quilting through the corners of every other block you get an uplifting feeling. Instead of just a simple straight line, we used a soft wavy line of stitching.

Be sure to tie on and tie off with a locking straight stitch at the beginning and ending of your stitching line. Do not back stitch. If you don't have a tie off stitch, change the stitch length to almost zero, then stitch in place for several stitches.

Set this Block aside and quilt it when you have assembled the Sampler Quilt. See pages 69 and 157-160.

Other Sparkling Bargello Ideas

This exciting Sulky quilted wallhanging was **designed by Patsy Shields, National Director of Education for Sulky of America.**

She added sparkle by using Lame' and quilting it with Sulky Sliver Metallic #8011.

Sulky "Sew Exciting" Seminar Vest 2

Designed by Joyce Drexler. The vest incorporates a "Random Bargello Technique" on the left lower section.

In Random Bargello, there are no matching seams. You actually do not want strips to line up exactly. Some creative yarns were couched over the Bargello on this vest using Sulky Polyester Smoke Invisible Thread. **See page 85-88 for steps on making another Random Bargello Quilt.**

For Information on Hosting a Sulky "Sew Exciting" Seminar for your Guild or group contact:

> **Sulky of America
> 3113 Broadpoint Drive
> Harbor Heights, FL 33983
> Fax: 1-941-743-4634
> E-mail: info@sulky.com**

Embroidered Random Bargello

"SNOWMEN ON ICE"
Shown by Carol Ingram on the PBS TV Show, AMERICA SEWS WITH SUE HAUSMANN
utilizes a background of random bargello using 15 various shades of blue. Each fabric was cut in random widths from 1-1/2" to 4", then sewn in sequence from dark to light, using a 1-1/2" burgundy red strip on either side of a very unique wintery fabric with flying geese. Doing so helped to showcase that fabric and reinforce the chevron pattern. The forest trees were raw-edge appliqued using mottled green Fossil fabric and Steam-A-Seam adhesive. They were scattered in sizes large and small to help create depth. Then they were free-motion stitched using Dark Green Sulky Ultra Twist #3002.

Carol's Designer Embroidery Cards #22 and #23 by Cactus Punch, allow you to play in the snow without the cold. Sulky 40 wt. Rayon Threads give the soft, beautiful sheen needed for a snowy scene. Carol gives extra dimension to the Snowmen's Hats and Scarves by using Sulky 2 mm Puffy Foam™ under the embroidery in selected areas. The quilt was stipple quilted with Sulky Opalescent Sliver #8040 and Silver Metallic #7001.

"INSPIRED WATERCOLOR WATER LILLY"
Also utilizes the Random Bargello technique along with the Amazing Designs Inspirational Concepts Embroidery Card # AD3000 **designed by Joyce Drexler. Quilted by Evelyn Howard using Sulky Sliver Opalescent #8040.**

Rail Fence

Created with 2 Sets of 3 Strips each.
"Uses the Strip Piecing Method".

*Using a 1/4" seam allowance is imperative. Press carefully - **DO NOT DISTORT STRIPS** as it will be very noticeable when the block is pieced.*

✂ *Cutting Guide*
Use the 6-1/2" Ruler

Always cut the selvages off the fabric before cutting strips.

✂ Cut two 1-1/2" x 44" strips - Color 1
✂ Cut one 1-1/2" x 44" strip - Color 2
✂ Cut one 1-1/2" x 44" strip - Color 3
✂ Cut one 1-1/2" x 44" strip - Color 4
✂ Cut one 1-1/2" x 44" strip - Color 5

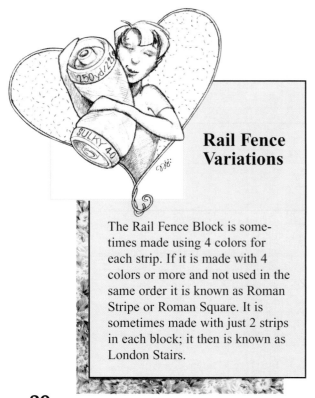

Rail Fence Variations

The Rail Fence Block is sometimes made using 4 colors for each strip. If it is made with 4 colors or more and not used in the same order it is known as Roman Stripe or Roman Square. It is sometimes made with just 2 strips in each block; it then is known as London Stairs.

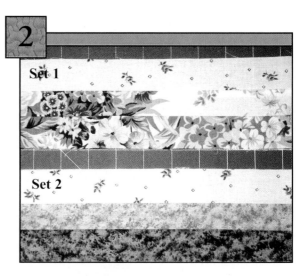

Set 1

Set 2

Sew 2 different Strip Sets of 3 Colors together in noted color order:

SET 1 - COLORS 1, 2 & 3.
SET 2 - COLORS 1, 4 & 5.

Press all seam allowances in one direction toward darkest color.

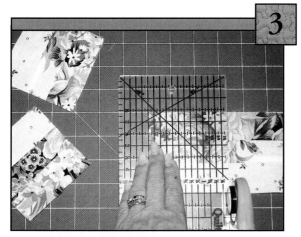

3

**CUT BOTH STRIPS INTO EXACT
3-1/2" SQUARES.**

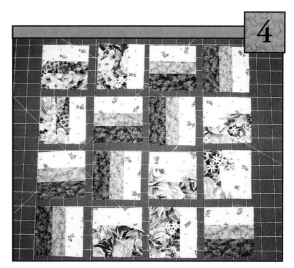

4

Lay out the 16 cross-cut 3-1/2" squares into
Rows 1 to 4 to make the Rail Fence design.
Set aside the unused squares for use in the
Cross Roads Variation Block. See page 46.

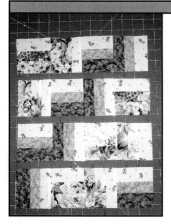

5

Sew the Sets into
4 Rows. Sew the
Rows into a
Finished Block
size 12-1/2"
square. Press
seam allowances
opposite to one
another. Use the
12-1/2" Quilter's
Square to
confirm Block
measurement.
Block if needed.

6

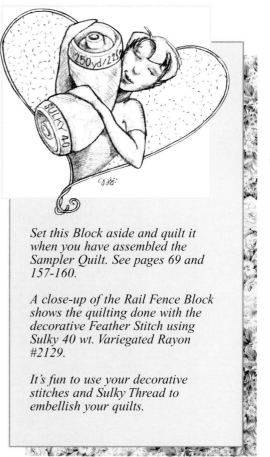

*Set this Block aside and quilt it
when you have assembled the
Sampler Quilt. See pages 69 and
157-160.*

*A close-up of the Rail Fence Block
shows the quilting done with the
decorative Feather Stitch using
Sulky 40 wt. Variegated Rayon
#2129.*

*It's fun to use your decorative
stitches and Sulky Thread to
embellish your quilts.*

DOWN ON THE FARM

Designed and Pieced by Marilyn Fisher Quilted by Evelyn Howard

Instead of always using the Rail Fence Blocks as your focal point, substitute a cute print the same size as the Rail Fence Block; "fussy cut" it (see page 48) using the small Quilter's Ruler to showcase the exact section of the fabric you want to use as your focal point. Quilted using 2 strands of Sulky 30 wt. Rayon #1071 Off-White in a serpentine 3.0 length on the Babylock Esante.

A Rail Fence with Sulky Applique

29" x 38"

What a different look you can achieve with a layer of Applique over your finished Rail Fence Blocks.

Mainly Batiks were chosen for this wall-hanging. The Butterfly inset squares are from Lee Ann Batiks. The large butterflies and leaf groupings were cut from a large panel. The Rail Fence block colors were chosen from colors in the batiks, and placed to represent a triple rail fence. The size of the blocks was determined by the size of the small batik butterfly squares. Sulky Puffy Foam was used under the inner wings of the large butterflies to give a raised 3-D effect.

Satin stitching with Sulky 30 wt. Multi-Color #2208 was done around the large butterfly's inner wings. The satin stitching around the outside of the butterflies was done with Sulky 30 wt. #1005 Black. Sulky Ultra Twist #3034 was used to quilt the fence rails with a machine feather stitch. The first border was quilted with Sulky Smoke Invisible. The outside border was quilted with Sulky Metallic #7022.

BUTTERFLIES ON MY RAIL FENCE

Designed, Pieced, Appliqued and Quilted by Marilyn Fisher

33

Spinning Star

Introduction of
4" Finished Half-Square
Triangles & Sulky KK 2000™

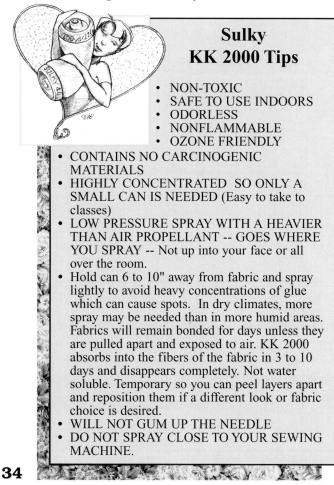

Sulky
KK 2000 Tips

- NON-TOXIC
- SAFE TO USE INDOORS
- ODORLESS
- NONFLAMMABLE
- OZONE FRIENDLY

- CONTAINS NO CARCINOGENIC MATERIALS
- HIGHLY CONCENTRATED SO ONLY A SMALL CAN IS NEEDED (Easy to take to classes)
- LOW PRESSURE SPRAY WITH A HEAVIER THAN AIR PROPELLANT -- GOES WHERE YOU SPRAY -- Not up into your face or all over the room.
- Hold can 6 to 10" away from fabric and spray lightly to avoid heavy concentrations of glue which can cause spots. In dry climates, more spray may be needed than in more humid areas. Fabrics will remain bonded for days unless they are pulled apart and exposed to air. KK 2000 absorbs into the fibers of the fabric in 3 to 10 days and disappears completely. Not water soluble. Temporary so you can peel layers apart and reposition them if a different look or fabric choice is desired.
- WILL NOT GUM UP THE NEEDLE
- DO NOT SPRAY CLOSE TO YOUR SEWING MACHINE.

1

✂ Cutting Guide
Use the 4-1/2" Ruler
Always cut the selvages off the fabric before cutting strips.

- ✂ Cut one 11" x 16" piece — Color 1
- ✂ Cut one 11" x 16" piece — Color 3
- ✂ Cut one 4-1/2" square — Color 3
- ✂ Cut one 4-1/2" x 22" strip — Color 4

Use one sheet of 4" Finished Half-Square Triangle Paper & Sulky KK 2000 Temporary Spray Adhesive

Use the two 11" x 16" fabrics that were cut above (Color 1 and Color 3).

Spray the Right Side of the darkest fabric with a light spray of KK 2000.

2

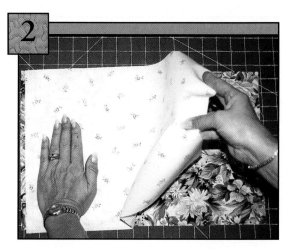

Putting right sides together, smooth the second, lighter fabric **Right Side Down** over the first fabric.

Lightly spray the Wrong Side of the second fabric.

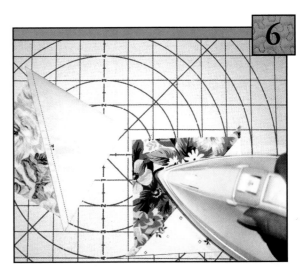

With the paper still on, press the seams to the darkest fabric.

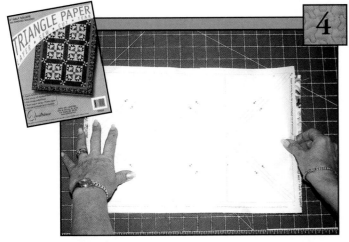

Smooth the 4" Finished Half-Square Triangle Paper over it making sure all layers are smooth.

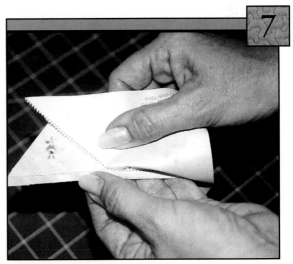

Remove the paper carefully by supporting the stitching with your finger and thumb as you pull the paper away with your other hand close to the stitching line.

Set aside 4 triangles to use in the "Hole in the Barn Door" Block on page 38.

Cut four 4-1/2" squares from the color #4 strip.

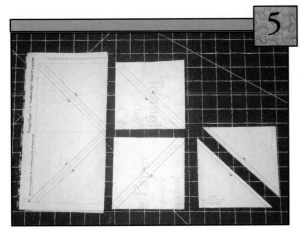

Shorten stitch length slightly to make it easier to remove the paper later. Begin sewing at the arrow at the top of the T-Paper.

Sew on the dotted lines in a continuous line. Then cut apart on the solid lines using your rotary cutter and ruler.

8

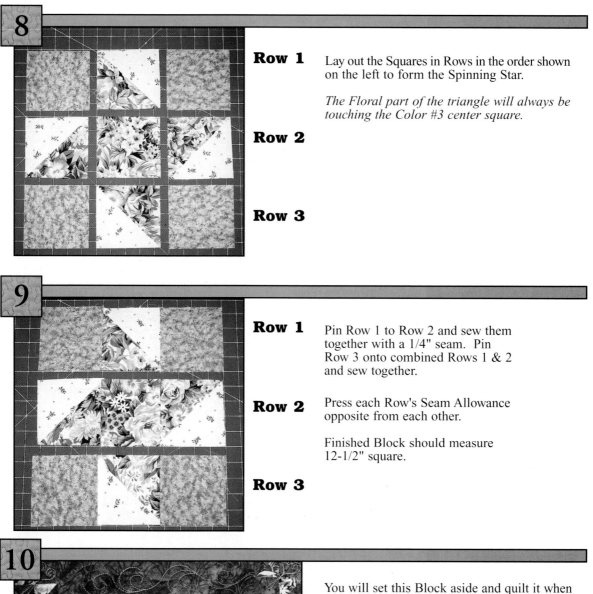

Row 1

Lay out the Squares in Rows in the order shown on the left to form the Spinning Star.

The Floral part of the triangle will always be touching the Color #3 center square.

Row 2

Row 3

9

Row 1

Pin Row 1 to Row 2 and sew them together with a 1/4" seam. Pin Row 3 onto combined Rows 1 & 2 and sew together.

Row 2

Press each Row's Seam Allowance opposite from each other.

Finished Block should measure 12-1/2" square.

Row 3

10

You will set this Block aside and quilt it when you have assembled the Sampler Quilt. See pages 69 and 157-160.

On The Garden Twist, Sulky Spinning Star Block you will be quilting "free-motion" in the ditch (see page 10) with Sulky Clear Invisible to stabilize the Block.

Then thread up with Sulky 30 wt. Rayon #2129. You will quilt "free-motion" (See page 55 for set-up for Free-Motion Quilting.) Stitch around the flowers in the center square.

Quilt all of Color 1 with a free-motion Serpentine Stitch.

Quilt in the Color #4 squares "free-motion" using the Rose Quilting pattern on page 72, traced onto Solvy.

Star Puzzle

Designed, Pieced and Quilted by Marilyn Fisher

Only 2 fabrics were used in making the design section of this wallhanging. It is composed of 3" half-square triangles, a 3" four-patch and a 3" square for the center of the stars. It is a Tessellation type of design.

The design part of the wallhanging was quilted very randomly using Sulky Sliver Metallic #8007 and #8020 and Sulky Original Metallic #7020. The border was quilted in loose, meandering, free-motion stitches using Sulky #7020 Metallic. The flower print is by Kona Bay Fabrics.

Ribbon Star

Designed, Pieced and Quilted by Marilyn Fisher

This wallhanging is composed of 3" half-square triangles plus a 3" square for the center of the star. They were set so they form a ribbon-like area around the star. The Star was quilted with loose, meandering, free-motion stitches using Sulky 30 wt. Rayon #1035. The first border was also quilted in the ditch with this same thread.

The blue ribbons were quilted with a straight stitch using Sulky 30 wt. Rayon #2104. The outside border was also quilted using this same variegated thread in very loose, meandering, free-motion stitches. The white print areas were quilted using Sulky Clear Invisible #0001 with a very tight free-motion stippling stitch.

37

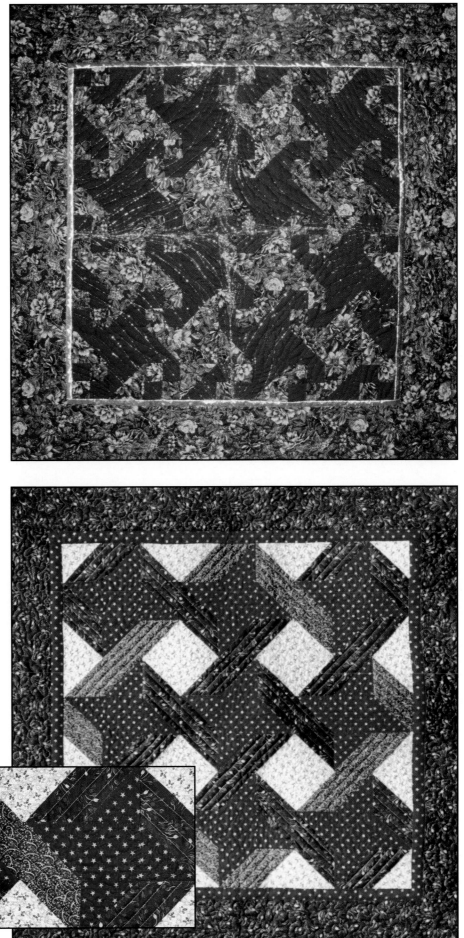

Hole in the Barn Door

A very pleasing block.
Simple to do and very versatile.

The Hole in the Barn Door has many names and variations. Other names include: Churn Dash, Monkey Wrench, Double Monkey Wrench, Sherman's March, and Barn Door. If a 4-patch is put in the strip sections, it is called Prairie Queen. If the colors are reversed on the strip sections, it is called Grecian Design. Sometimes this block has an 8 point star in the center.

1

✂ Cutting Guide
Use the 4-1/2" Ruler

Always cut the selvages off the fabric before cutting strips.

✂ Cut one 2-1/2" x 22" strip - Color 1
✂ Cut one 2-1/2" x 22" strip - Color 3
✂ Cut one 4-1/2" square - Color 2

Use the 4 remaining half-square triangles from
The Spinning Star on page 34.

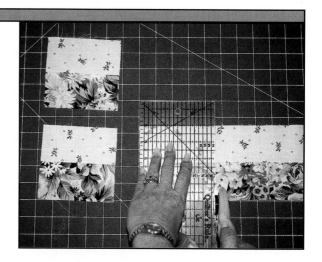

Using a 1/4" seam allowance, sew together the 2-1/2" x 22" strips of Color 1 and Color 3 fabrics. Cut four 4-1/2" squares from this combined Strip Set.

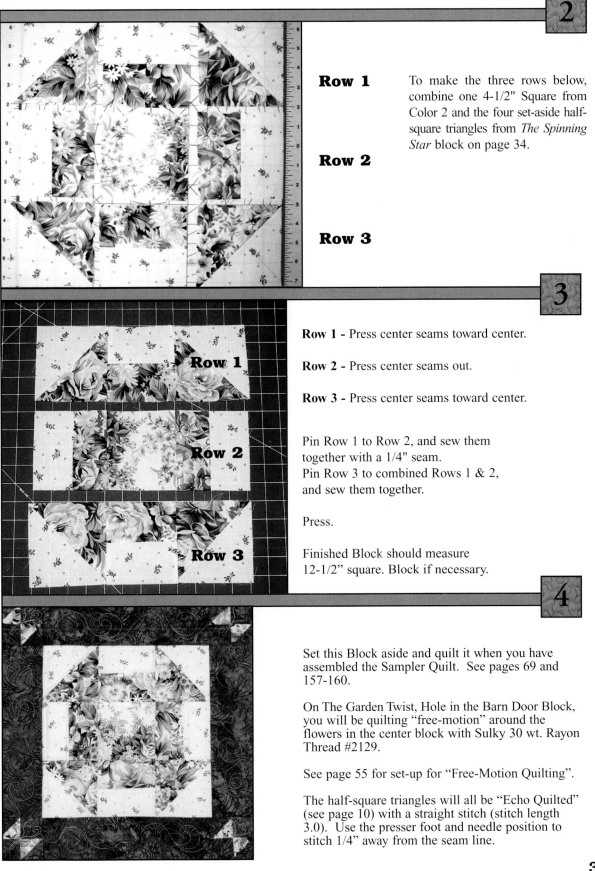

2

Row 1

Row 2

Row 3

To make the three rows below, combine one 4-1/2" Square from Color 2 and the four set-aside half-square triangles from *The Spinning Star* block on page 34.

3

Row 1 - Press center seams toward center.

Row 2 - Press center seams out.

Row 3 - Press center seams toward center.

Pin Row 1 to Row 2, and sew them together with a 1/4" seam.
Pin Row 3 to combined Rows 1 & 2, and sew them together.

Press.

Finished Block should measure 12-1/2" square. Block if necessary.

4

Set this Block aside and quilt it when you have assembled the Sampler Quilt. See pages 69 and 157-160.

On The Garden Twist, Hole in the Barn Door Block, you will be quilting "free-motion" around the flowers in the center block with Sulky 30 wt. Rayon Thread #2129.

See page 55 for set-up for "Free-Motion Quilting".

The half-square triangles will all be "Echo Quilted" (see page 10) with a straight stitch (stitch length 3.0). Use the presser foot and needle position to stitch 1/4" away from the seam line.

▲ *Cows in the Pasture*

Both Quilts were Designed and Pieced by Marilyn Fisher and Quilted by Evelyn Howard.
"Cows in the Pasture" was quilted with Sulky Ultra Twist™ Rayon Thread #3040.

Another fun *Hole in the Barn Door Quilt* is this one featuring Bunny Prints in the center square of the block, quilted with Sulky 30 wt. Rayon #1046 Teal, #1192 ▶ Fuchsia and #1071 Off-White. Make the center square your focal point or theme area. If you have a computerized embroidery machine, why not embroider a series of designs for this area using soft, warm and natural-looking Sulky 40 wt. Rayon Thread?

Are there Bunnies in the Barn?

Tail of Benjamin's Kite

Introduction of an
Alternative Method for making
Triangles without Triangle Paper.

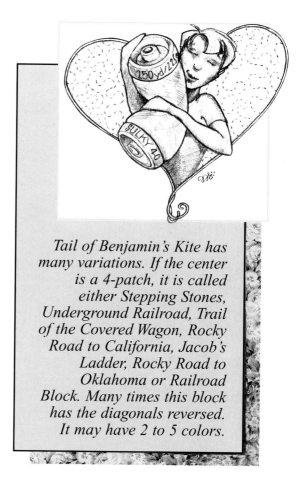

Tail of Benjamin's Kite has many variations. If the center is a 4-patch, it is called either Stepping Stones, Underground Railroad, Trail of the Covered Wagon, Rocky Road to California, Jacob's Ladder, Rocky Road to Oklahoma or Railroad Block. Many times this block has the diagonals reversed. It may have 2 to 5 colors.

1

✂ Cutting Guide

Use both the 4-1/2" & 6-1/2" Quilter's Rulers

Always cut the selvages off the fabric before cutting strips.

✂ Cut one 4-7/8" x 22" strip - Color 1
✂ Cut one 4-7/8" x 22" strip - Color 6
✂ Cut one 4-1/2" square   - Color 3
✂ Cut two 2-1/2" x 22" strips - Color 2
✂ Cut two 2-1/2" x 22" strips - Color 4

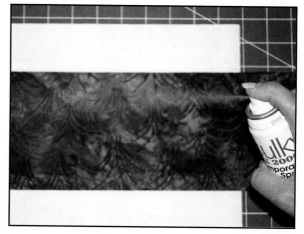

Place a sheet of paper on the cutting mat or table top to protect it from the spray of the KK 2000 Temporary Spray Adhesive. Lay the Color 6 strip right side up and lightly spray it with KK 2000 while holding the can 6 to 10" away from the fabric.

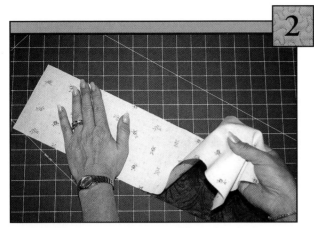

With Color 6 strip right side up, lay the Color 1 strip right side down (right sides together), over the Color 6 strip. Starting at one end, smooth it with your hand as you lay the strip down.

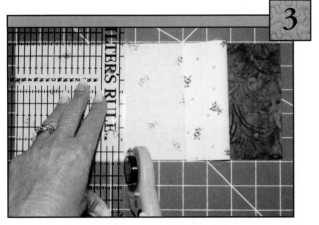

Using the large 6-1/2" Quilter's Ruler, cut four 4-7/8" squares from the glued-together strip.

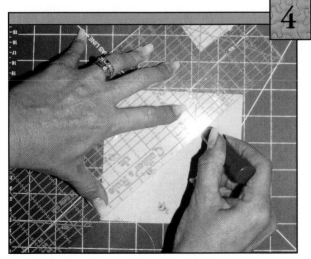

Using the smaller 4-1/2" Quilter's Ruler and a Clover Rolling Chalk Marker, draw a diagonal line from corner to corner on all of the glued-together squares.

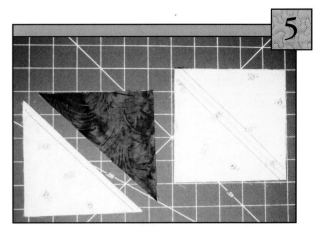

With a short stitch length, sew a straight stitch 1/4" away from each side of the drawn line. Using your 4-1/2" Quilter's Ruler and a rotary cutter and mat, cut along the drawn line making 2 sets of triangles from each square.

Lay the Color 2 strip right side down over the Color 4 strip, matching raw edges. Sew together along the long side using a 1/4" seam allowance. Press seam allowance toward the Color 4 Strip. Cut eight 2-1/2" x 4-1/2" sets from the sewn-together strip.

Construct the 4-Patch Block. Lay paired sets so colors are opposite one another with the seams nesting together. Pin and sew using a 1/4" seam allowance.

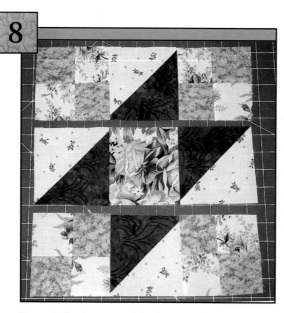

8

Lay out the Tail of Benjamin's Kite Block in three rows for easy construction, placing the 4-1/2" square of Color 3 in the center.

Match seams, pin and sew together with a 1/4" seam allowance.

Press the top and bottom row seam allowances toward the corner blocks, and the middle row toward the middle block.

Measure the Block with a 12-1/2" Quilter's Square to be sure your Block is 12-1/2" square.

If needed, place your block on a pin board that shows the desired 12-1/2" square measurement, or draw a 12-1/2" block on your pin board.

Lightly mist the Block and press while easing the block to the correct size. Pin. Press dry.

9

Holly Sash

Continuous Line Holly Sash Design by Hari Walner from her Celebration Series.

Begin Stitching Here

Set this Block aside and quilt it when you have assembled the Sampler Quilt. See pages 69 and 157-160.

On The Garden Twist, Tail of Benjamin's Kite Block, you will be quilting "free-motion" in the ditch (see page 10) with Sulky Clear Invisible Thread to stabilize the block. Then, with Sulky 30 wt. Rayon #2129, you will quilt "free-motion" around the flowers in the center block. See page 55 for set-up for Free-Motion Quilting. The half-square triangles will all be quilted in Color 1 with a free-motion serpentine stitch, and the 4-patch corner blocks will be quilted with a machine-fed straight stitch (3.0 stitch length setting) from corner to corner.

This lovely Christmas Quilt and matching Pillow uses the Benjamin's Kite Block repeated and sashed. Patti chose to feature computerized embroidery Christmas Designs from the New Home Memory Cards #109 & 110. Patti quilted an "X" across the flowers' and leaves' blocks with Sulky Sliver Metallic Thread #8007 Gold. She stipple quilted with Sulky Ultra Twist #3006 inside the center squares to make the embroidered designs pop!

The embroidery designs were done using Sulky 40 wt. Rayon Threads with 4 layers of Sulky Tear-Easy under the 100% cotton quilt square so no puckers were created; each layer tore away easily without distorting the design or tearing the threads.

In the border and sashing, she featured the Continuous Line Holly Sash Quilt Design by Hari Walner from her "Celebration Collection" (See previous page). It can be easily repeated using the Sulky Iron-on Transfer Pen on Sulky Tear-Easy Stabilizer.

A Sulky Holly-Days Christmas

Designed, Pieced and Quilted by Patti Lee

Fabrics: A Hoffman Christmas Collection.

Because Patti wanted to enlarge the sashing and border design by 21% to 41%, she cut Sulky Tear-Easy into 8-1/2" x 11" sheets, sprayed them with KK-2000 and smoothed them onto regular copy machine paper, which she ran through a copy machine to make "Tear-Easy" patterns just the perfect size for the sashings and borders.

45

Cross Roads Variation

Introduction of 3" Finished Half-Square Triangular Paper

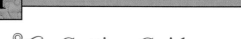

✂ Cutting Guide

Use the 6-1/2" Quilter's Ruler

Always cut the selvages off the fabric before cutting strips.

✂ Cut one 9" x 16-1/2" piece - Color 1
✂ Cut one 9" x 16-1/2" piece - Color 6
✂ Cut one 3-1/2" x 22" strip - Color 3

Use eight leftover 3-1/2" squares from the Rail Fence Block on page 30.

The Original Arkansas Cross Roads Variation had solid squares one way and print squares where we have placed the striped squares. We wanted to use the squares left over from the Rail Fence Block, so we called it a variation. When this same block is made using all solids in 2 colors, it is called Road to Oklahoma.

2

Following the directions for using triangle paper in the Spinning Star Block on pages 34 & 35, use the finished 3" triangle paper, layering Color 6 and Color 1 with KK 2000 in between to make the Triangles for Cross Roads Variation.

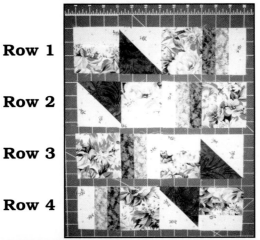

Row 1

Row 2

Row 3

Row 4

Cut four 3-1/2" squares of Color 3. Lay out the block in 4 rows for easy construction.

Pick up two abutting pieces at a time from your layout and sew them together using a 1/4" seam allowance.

Press seams to one side.

Your finished block should measure 12-1/2" square.

Set this Block aside and quilt it when you have assembled the Sampler Quilt.
See pages 69 and 157-160.

On The Garden Twist, Cross Roads Variation Block, you will be quilting "free-motion" in the ditch (see page 10) with Sulky Clear Invisible Thread to stabilize the Block.

Then, you will use Sulky 30 wt. Rayon #2129 to quilt "free-motion" (see page 55 for set-up for Free-Motion Quilting).

The half-square triangles will all be quilted in Color 1 with a "free-motion" Serpentine Stitch. The solid floral squares (color #3) will be quilted over a Solvy Pattern of the Rose Design found on page 72.

The Rail Fence Blocks will be quilted with a machine-fed decorative Feather Stitch.

47

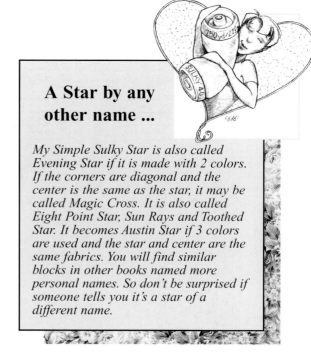

My Simple Sulky Star

Introduction of Squares and Rectangles to make Triangles

1

✂ Cutting Guide

Use both the 4-1/2" & 6-1/2" Quilter's Rulers

Always cut the selvages off the fabric before cutting strips.

✂ Fussy cut one 6-1/2" square   - Color 2
    Fussy cut means to place the exact-size ruler over the exact area of the fabric you want to feature and cut out just that area.
✂ Cut four 3-1/2" x 6-1/2" strips   - Color 1
✂ Cut four 3-1/2" squares   - Color 1
✂ Cut eight 3-1/2" squares   - Color 3

Place the first Color 3 Square, **right side down**, on one of the sprayed corners of the Color 1 Rectangle. ▶

Using the small Ruler and a Clover Rolling Blue Chalk Marker, draw a line from corner to corner of the 3" square.

▲ Spray KK 2000 on the upper left and upper right corners of the **right side** of Color 1 Rectangles.

2

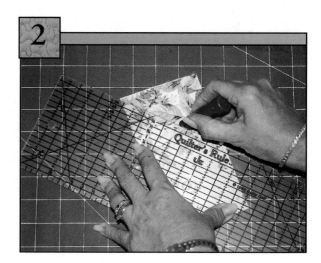

3

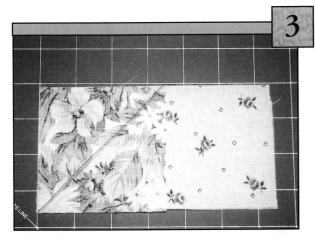

Sew a straight line just inside the chalk line, not on it.

4

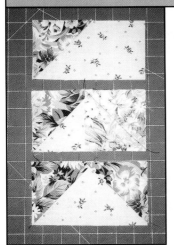

Fold the Square back on itself to create the Triangle.

This method eliminates the seam line on Color 1.

Repeat Steps 2-4 to put the second square on the other sprayed corner and two Color 3 squares on each of the other three Color 1 rectangles.

5

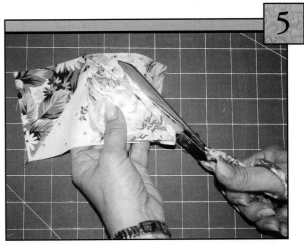

Fold the top layer of the Triangle Square out of the way and **trim away the under Triangle of Color 3, leaving a 1/4" seam allowance to reduce bulk. To maintain the integrity of the original Rectangle, do not trim away Color 1.**

6

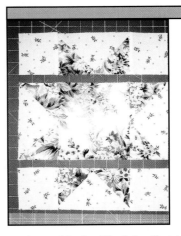

ROW 1

ROW 2

ROW 3

Assemble the Block by first laying out the piece in three rows. Stitch the three rows together, one row at a time to form the Block. Press toward center block. Measure to be sure it is 12-1/2" square.

7

Set this Block aside and quilt it when you have assembled the Sampler Quilt. See pages 69 and 157-160.

On The Garden Twist, Sulky Simple Star Block you will be quilting "free-motion" in the ditch (see page 10) with Sulky Clear Invisible Thread to stabilize the Block.

Then you will use Sulky 30 wt. Rayon #2129 to quilt "Free-Motion" (see page 55 for set-up for Free-Motion Quilting). Stitch around the flowers in the center square.

Quilt all of Color 1 with a free-motion serpentine stitch.

Joyce Drexler's Sulky Inspirations

Both quilts were designed by Joyce Drexler using the Computerized Embroidery Card #AD3000 "Inspirational Concepts in Sulky" which she designed for Amazing Designs™. The Embroidery Card has 20 different Floral Designs with inspirational messages on each.

The Wallhanging to the left, quilted by Evelyn Howard, was shown on the PBS TV Show, "Martha's Sewing Room" with Martha Pullen. It used the block, "Double X Variation" as shown on pages 58 and 59. Using the wire hanger from Michell Marketing really added a homey touch.

The quilt to the right used the Simple Star Block but with inverted outside points to make a frame around the center square. Designs were embroidered using Sulky 40 wt. Rayon with 4 layers of Sulky Tear-Easy (sprayed with KK 2000 with 2 layers of Tear-Easy going in one direction and 2 in another). When removing Tear-Easy, tear off each layer separately by pulling it away from the supported embroidery to avoid stretching the fabric or distorting the embroidery.

All were quilted using Sulky 30 wt. Rayon in solid or variegated shades.

As seen on the "Sew Creative" PBS TV Show with Donna Wilder.

Garments embroidered with Sulky 40 wt. Rayon Thread featuring "Inspirational Concepts" created by Evelyn Howard for Joyce Drexler.

Starring Sulky Twisted Fruits

Featuring the "Fruit" Card #33 by Brother.

Embroidered using both Sulky Ultra Twist™ Thread and Sulky 30 wt. Rayon through a single size 16/100 denim machine needle to achieve a special blending of threads for a very natural, soft look of hand crewel.

Quilted with Sulky Ultra Twist Rayon #3025 and Sulky 30 wt. Rayon #1082, using both strands through one 90/14 embroidery needle.

Designed and Quilted by Joyce Drexler
Embroidery by Jan Ambers.

Stars of First Grade

Designed, Pieced, and Quilted by Marilyn Fisher using Sulky Sliver Metallic #8020, Sulky 40 wt. #1001 and Sulky Polyester Clear Invisible.

46" x 61"

Fabrics by Alexander Henry, Benartex and Hoffman.

Kansas Troubles

There will be *no trouble* at all if you note the placement of the triangles. The top left and bottom right triangles sit in a different direction than the others. When you look at the finished quilts (pages 56 & 57) that use just this block repeated throughout, you can see the importance of the layout of the triangles. Alternate the direction of the blocks as well. Use your favorite fabric from your stash for the main fabric but include a strong contrasting solid in the triangles.

It is also the perfect block to support a large, free-motion or computerized embroidery motif. Let your imagination go wild and Kansas Troubles may become your favorite quilt block.

1

✄ Cutting Guide

Use the 6-1/2" Quilter's Ruler

Always cut the selvages off the fabric before cutting strips.

✄ Fussy cut (see page 48)
    one 9-1/2" square   - Color 2
✄ Cut one 3-1/2" square   - Color 2
✄ Cut one 9-1/2" x 16-1/2" piece - Color 2
✄ Cut one 9-1/2" x 16-1/2" piece - Color 6

Supplies

- 1 Sheet of 3" Finished Triangle Paper
- Sulky KK 2000 Temporary Spray Adhesive

Use the KK 2000 method (pages 34 & 35) with the 9-1/2" x 16-1/2" pieces of Color 2 and Color 6 to make one sheet of Triangles with the 3" Finished Triangle Paper.

Lay out the Block as photo shows,
sewing a row of triangles for Row 1.
Be mindful of which way you have turned the
corner triangles. This is really the only *"trouble"*
in this Kansas Troubles Block.

Sew Row 1 to the 9-1/2" square of Color 2. Be sure the fabric print is turned to best show off the design.
Then join another row of triangles and one 3-1/2" square of Color 2 to the rest of the Block to finish.

Set this Block aside and quilt it when you have assembled the
Sampler Quilt. See pages 69 and 157-160.

General Instructions to Set up for Free-motion Quilting:

1. Lower or cover Feed Dogs.
2. Loosen the Top Tension slightly.
3. Select the Straight Stitch.
4. Insert a size 90 Quilting Needle.
5. Attach a darning foot.
6. Make sure the machine is properly threaded by lowering the presser bar and pulling down on the top thread just above the needle. If the thread pulls through easily with no resistance, re-thread the top and check it again until you feel resistance.
7. Bring up the bobbin thread through the quilt. Hold on to both threads securely as you begin to stitch.

On this project, free-motion stitch around the flowers and leaves of the center print using 30 wt. #2129.

Echo Quilt (see page 10) the Triangles 1/4" from the seam line with a machine-fed straight stitch using the presser foot as a guide.

No Troubles with Sulky

Pieced by Joyce Drexler and Quilted by Tina Ignatowicz on a long-arm quilting machine using Multi-Color Sulky 30 wt. Rayon #2210.

Isn't it interesting how the blocks are arranged to develop a secondary pattern?

The black mottled fabric is by Moda, while the floral is by South Seas Imports.

Quilted over Fairfield's Low-Loft Polyester Batting.

Joyce pieced this quilt with her "Half-Wits" Quilting Group in Milwaukee, WI at Hearthside Quilter's Nook. They meet every 6 months when Joyce is in Milwaukee taping PBS TV Sewing Shows.

Carolina Dreaming

**Patti Lee Pieced and Quilted this Kansas Troubles Quilt using Sulky Ultra Twist #3045
and Sulky Variegated 30 wt. Rayon #2135.** She also used the Continuous Line Quilting Pattern "Leaping
Leaves" and "Young Oak" from the Borders & Corners Collection by Hari Walner.
(See pull-out pattern sheet.) Fabric: Hoffman Batiks

Double "X" Variation

Another easy Block using leftovers from Cross Roads Variation.

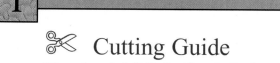

☒ **Cutting Guide**
Use the 6-1/2" Quilter's Ruler

**Always cut the selvages off the fabric
before cutting strips.**

✂ Fussy cut (see page 48)
     one 6-1/2" square   - Color 2
✂ Cut two 3-1/2" squares   - Color 3
✂ Cut one 9-1/2" x 16-1/2" piece - Color 1
✂ Cut one 9-1/2" x 16-1/2" piece - Color 4

**Use Leftover Triangles of Color 1 & Color 6
from Cross Roads Variation Block page 46.**

You will also need:
1 Sheet of 3" Finished Triangle Paper
KK 2000 Temporary Spray Adhesive

The original Double "X" Block has only 3 sections across. We added another one because we wanted a large center section to use as a focal point. Sometimes it is desirable to change a traditional block to suit a purpose. It's perfectly all right to do this, and when you do, simply name it a Variation of the original block name. If you spend any time looking through quilt books, you will probably find a block similar to the way you have changed it. Today, there are numerous quilt books available in which traditional blocks have been changed and rechanged many times until they are really a new block and not a variation any longer.

Use the KK 2000 method to make Triangles with the 3" Finished Triangle Paper and the 9-1/2" x 16-1/2" pieces of Color 1 and Color 4. (See pages 34 and 35.)

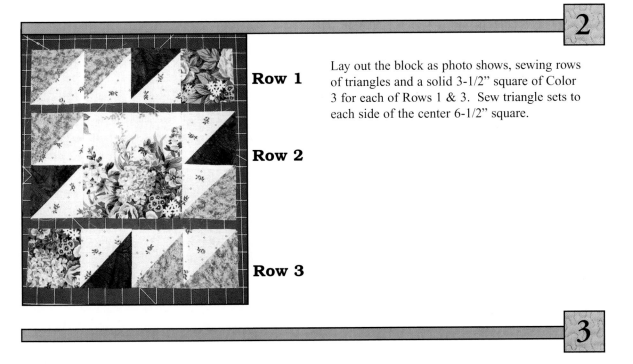

Row 1

Row 2

Row 3

Lay out the block as photo shows, sewing rows of triangles and a solid 3-1/2" square of Color 3 for each of Rows 1 & 3. Sew triangle sets to each side of the center 6-1/2" square.

Set this Block aside and quilt it when you have assembled the Sampler Quilt. See pages 69 and 157-160.

On The Garden Twist, Double "X" Variation Block, you will be quilting "free-motion" in the ditch (see page 10) with Sulky Clear Invisible Thread to stabilize the block.

Then, with Sulky 30 wt. Rayon #2129, you will quilt "free-motion" around the flowers in the center block. See page 55 for set-up for Free-Motion Quilting.

The half-square triangles will all be "Echo Quilted" (see page 10) with a straight stitch (stitch length 3.0). Use the presser foot and needle position to stitch 1/4" away from the seam line.

Sulky House

Introduction to Foundation Piecing on Sulky Tear-Easy Stabilizer

House pattern located on pull-out pattern sheet.

1

✂ Cutting Guide
Use the 4-1/2" Quilter's Rule

Always cut the selvages off the fabric before cutting strips.

✂ Cut one 4" x 22-1/2" strip - Color 1
✂ Cut one 3" x 45" strip   - Color 2
✂ Cut one 4" x 45" strip   - Color 4
✂ Cut one 5" x 22-1/2" strip - Color 5
✂ Cut one 2-1/2" x 15" strip - Color 6
   Or just use your scraps of these colors.
✂ Cut one 12" x 12" square of Tear-Easy

Getting Started:

1. On the pull-out pattern sheet, the pieces in the block are numbered to indicate the stitching sequence.
2. The Color Number of each fabric is also indicated.
3. There are two pieced units that have to be done alone, then incorporated into the design.
4. Always cut your pieces larger than the space they will cover to allow for seam allowances. You can pre-cut your fabric pieces to speed up production of the blocks once you know the size needed.
5. Use your rotary cutter, mat and 4-1/2" quilter's ruler to trim seam allowances to an exact 1/4". This is more important when using light fabrics that you will see through.
6. Set your straight stitch length to 18 stitches per inch and use a larger needle size than normal to help in perforating the Tear-Easy.
7. You will always place the fabric to the unmarked side of the Tear-Easy.

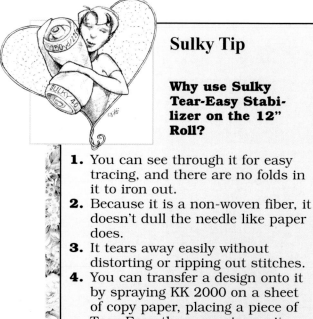

Sulky Tip

Why use Sulky Tear-Easy Stabilizer on the 12" Roll?

1. You can see through it for easy tracing, and there are no folds in it to iron out.
2. Because it is a non-woven fiber, it doesn't dull the needle like paper does.
3. It tears away easily without distorting or ripping out stitches.
4. You can transfer a design onto it by spraying KK 2000 on a sheet of copy paper, placing a piece of Tear-Easy the same size on it, and running it through a copier. Since copy machines may change the size of the design by 1/16" overall, if you are making multiples of one design in a project, make all of them on the copier.

Why KK 2000?
It makes tracing a breeze by keeping the design and the Tear-Easy from shifting while tracing. It is also ideal for holding fabric pieces in place without pins so you can stitch them.

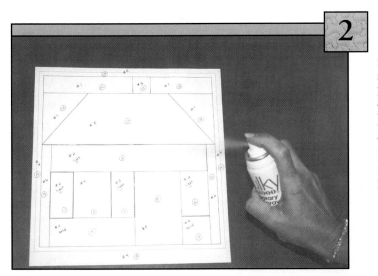

Spray KK 2000 onto either the design side of the house pattern (from the pull-out pattern sheet) or either side of a 12" square of Tear-Easy; adhere them together. This makes tracing a breeze by keeping the design and the Tear-Easy from shifting while tracing. KK 2000 is also ideal for holding fabric pieces in place without pins so you can stitch them.

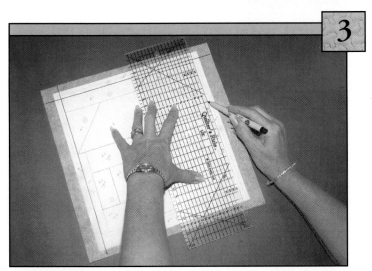

To create your sewing line, use a permanent-ink, fine-line marker and a ruler to trace the house design onto the Tear-Easy. Your finished block will only be as straight and even as these lines are drawn. If you need multiples, trace the design (flipped to back side) onto a piece of paper with a Sulky Iron-On Transfer Pen. Then, use a hot iron to transfer it onto as many squares of Tear-Easy as desired. After transferring, add sequence numbers and color numbers from the pattern (see page 17 for color number key) using a permanent-ink, fine-line marker so they are readable from the stitching side.

Add fabrics according to sequence numbers.

ADD PIECE #1 - Color 2 (lighter floral area)

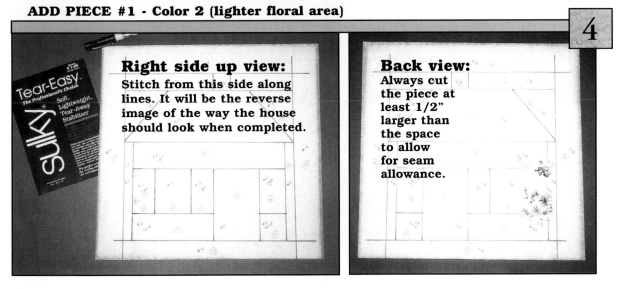

Right side up view:
Stitch from this side along lines. It will be the reverse image of the way the house should look when completed.

Back view:
Always cut the piece at least 1/2" larger than the space to allow for seam allowance.

Here's how to begin: Lay your first strip of Color 2 fabric under the section labeled #1 so it extends beyond all the lines at least 1/4". Lightly spray the wrong side of this piece with KK 2000 before placing it so it will stay in place and make it easier to sew the next piece.

5 **ADD PIECES #2 & #3 - Colors 4 & 2 (lighter floral area)**

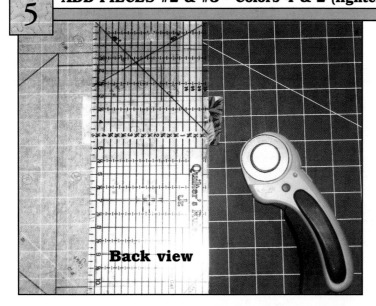

Back view

As each piece is added, trim to a 1/4" seam allowance and press.

Some people call this a "flip and sew method", since you are constantly flipping the Tear-Easy Foundation over to place a fabric, right sides together, and then flipping the Tear-Easy Foundation back to stitch the seam.

The easiest way to trim to a perfect 1/4" seam allowance is by folding the foundation out of the way, exposing only the raw edges of the fabric you wish to trim, then lining up your 4-1/2" ruler with the first 1/4" line over the stitched seam line, and trimming with a rotary cutter and mat.

Or you may prefer to trim with scissors.

6 **ADD PIECE #4 - Color 2 (bolder floral area)**

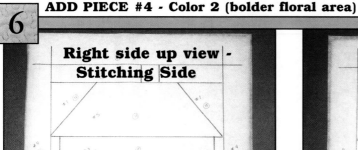

Right side up view - Stitching Side

Back view

7 **ADD PIECE #5 - Color 5**

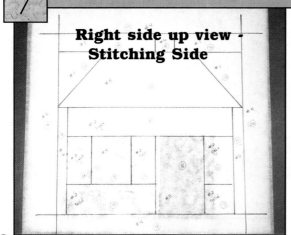
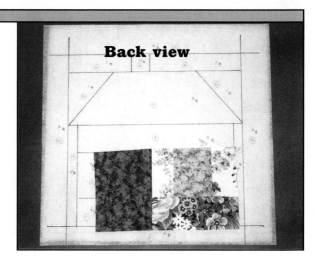

Right side up view - Stitching Side

Back view

ADD PIECES #6 & #7 - Colors 2 (one bolder and one lighter floral)

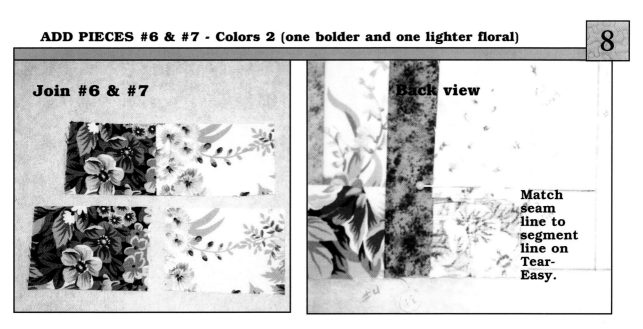

Join #6 & #7

Back view

Match seam line to segment line on Tear-Easy.

ADD PIECES #6 & #7 Continued

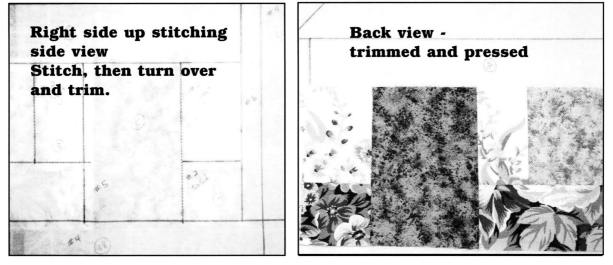

Right side up stitching side view
Stitch, then turn over and trim.

Back view - trimmed and pressed

ADD PIECE #8 - Color 2
(lighter floral)
Stitched & Trimmed

ADD PIECES #9 & #10 - Color 6

Right side up view - stitching side

Back view - pressed

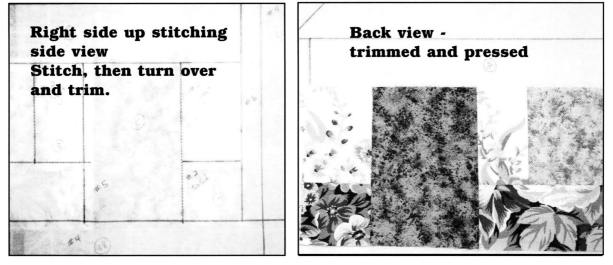

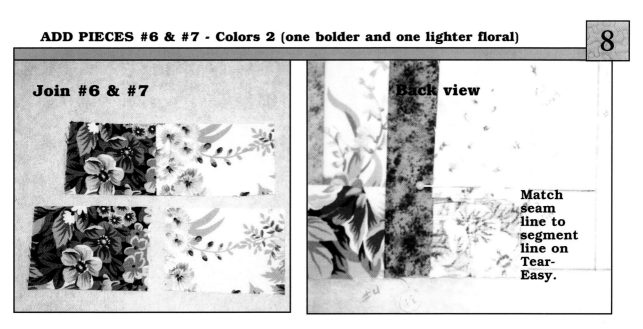

10 ADD PIECE #11 - Color 5

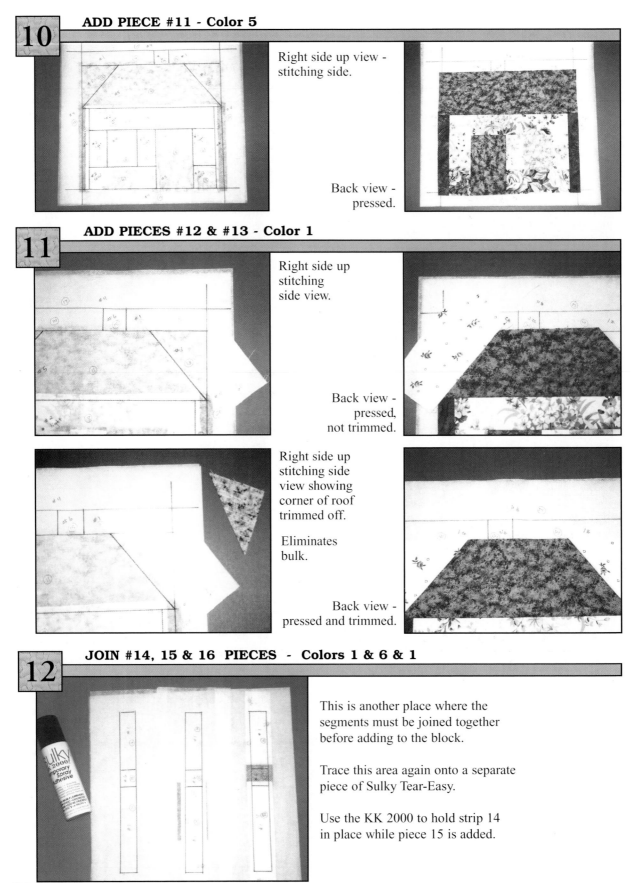

Right side up view - stitching side.

Back view - pressed.

11 ADD PIECES #12 & #13 - Color 1

Right side up stitching side view.

Back view - pressed, not trimmed.

Right side up stitching side view showing corner of roof trimmed off.

Eliminates bulk.

Back view - pressed and trimmed.

12 JOIN #14, 15 & 16 PIECES - Colors 1 & 6 & 1

This is another place where the segments must be joined together before adding to the block.

Trace this area again onto a separate piece of Sulky Tear-Easy.

Use the KK 2000 to hold strip 14 in place while piece 15 is added.

ADD PIECE #16

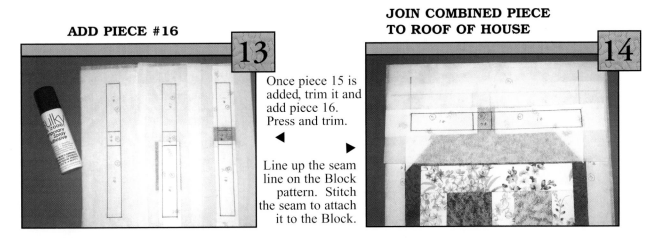

13

Once piece 15 is added, trim it and add piece 16. Press and trim.

◀   ▶

Line up the seam line on the Block pattern. Stitch the seam to attach it to the Block.

JOIN COMBINED PIECE TO ROOF OF HOUSE

14

REMOVE THE TEAR-EASY

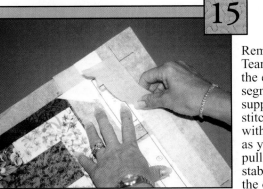

15

Remove the Tear-Easy from the extra added segment by supporting the stitching line with one hand as you gently pull away the stabilizer with the other hand.

PRESS AND TRIM

16

ADD PIECES #17 THROUGH #20 - Color 4

17

Make sure you cut your border strips a little wider than usual so they can be trimmed down to the Block Finished Size of 12-1/2" square.

REMOVE TEAR-EASY

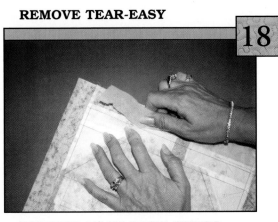

18

REMOVE TEAR-EASY, PRESS AND TRIM TO FINISHED SIZE

Remove the rest of the Tear-Easy Stabilizer. Press and trim to finished size of 12-1/2" square.

19

The floral print collection didn't lend itself to further decorating because the floral fabric added the flowers needed, but we decorated the Cherrywood Fabric House Block below.

If you know how to do silk ribbon embroidery by machine or by hand, you could substitute the zig-zagged, bar-tacked flowers for flowers of ribbon. *Have fun with it.*

Before embellishing the House Block, "stitch in the ditch" (see page 10) around the outside of the house, roof, door, etc. with Sulky Smoke Invisible Thread to stabilize the block and keep the elements of the inside of the block from getting out of shape.

Shingles -
1 Thread of Sulky Ultra Twist #3030 using a built-in Scallop Stitch. Use the presser foot as a guide to keep the rows of stitching evenly spaced and straight.

Door & Outside of Window -
2 Threads of Ultra Twist #3030 using a built-in Saddle Stitch. If you do not have a Saddle Stitch, set your stitch width to zero and use your multiple zig-zag stitch.

Outside Green Border -
Same as the door above only use 2 threads of Ultra Twist #3040. Echo Quilt 1/4" from the inside edge.

Flower Box, Chimney and Curtains -
Two strands of Sulky Ultra Twist #3006 through one size 90 needle. The "x" in the flower pots and chimney were stitched with one strand in the needle.

Sheers in Window -
Sliver #8020 in a built-in Honeycomb Stitch.

Leaves -
One strand of Sulky Ultra Twist #3030. Built-in Decorative Leaf Stitch.

The Flowers - To make the zig-zag flowers, put one strand of Sulky Sliver #8033 and one strand of Ultra Twist #3013 through one needle, lower the feed dogs and simply zig-zag in place 4-6 times, ending where you wish the center of the flower to be each time before pivoting the fabric to create the next petal. Vary the width of the zig-zag for different sized flowers. Be sure to tie on and tie off or bury your thread ends.

Butterfly Cornerstones in the Sashing & Borders

It's easy to make Butterflies using Triangle Paper.
Use 1-1/2" Finished for Sashing and 3-1/2" Finished for Borders

1

✂ Cutting Guide

Always cut the selvages off the fabric before cutting strips.

✂ Cut two 10-1/2" x 16-1/2" rectangles — - Color 3
✂ Cut two 10-1/2" x 16-1/2" rectangles — - Color 6
  to use with 1-1/2" and 3-1/2" Finished Triangle Paper
✂ Cut 31 3-1/2" x 12-1/2" strips for Sashing — - Color 6
✂ Cut six 2" x 45" strips for Accent Border — - Color 3
✂ Cut five 7-1/2" x 45" strips for Border — - Color 6
✂ Cut two 2" x 45" strips for Sashing Butterflies - Color 6
✂ Cut one 4" x 45" strip for Border Butterflies — - Color 6

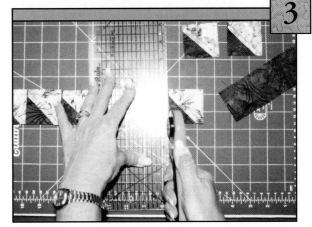

Press the triangles open toward Color 6.
Remove the triangle paper after pressing.

2

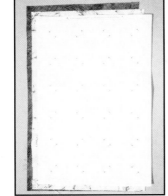

Prepare and stitch the two triangle papers using Colors 6 & 3. Place Color 6 right side up and spray it with KK 2000. Smooth Color 3 right side down over Color 6. Spray the wrong side of Color 3 with KK 2000 and smooth the Triangle Paper over it. Stitch along the dotted lines. Cut apart on the solid lines.

3

Sew the half-square triangles to a 2" strip of Color 6, snugly butting the half-square triangles close together. By sewing them to each strip rather than to individual squares, you will save time and have more accurate squares when you cut them apart after pressing. Cut apart with a rotary cutter, mat and ruler; then press.

67

4

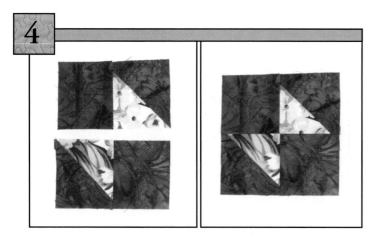

Sew the combined triangle and Color 6 rectangle to another combined set to form the Butterfly square.

5

Lay out the Blocks in the order they will be in the quilt. Sew the 3-1/2" x 12-1/2" Sashing to the blocks in horizontal rows.

6

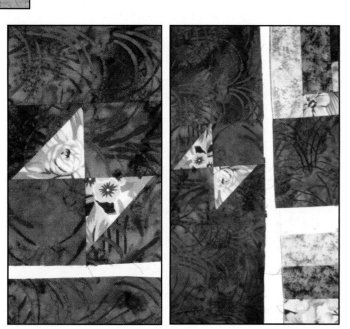

7

Place the Butterflies so they point into the quilt.

8

Measure the center of the quilt to get the proper measurement for the Accent Border Strips of Color 3. (This is illustrated in the "Borders" section on page 159.) Add the 2" wide, Color 3 Accent Border.

Repeat steps 1-4, using the 4" x 45" strips to create the wide Butterfly Corners with the 3-1/2" Finished Butterflies to accent the wide Color 6 Borders.

← Sew the Butterfly Square to the 3-1/2" x 12-1/2" strips of Sashing to form the vertical rows.

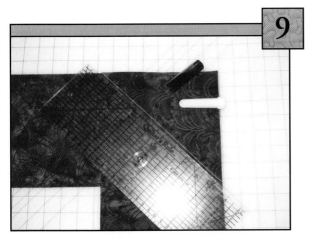

If you have to piece the Border strips to get the length needed, lay the strip to be added (extending 1/4" beyond the other), right side down perpendicular (90° angle) over the strip you are adding to.

Draw a line, left to right, using your ruler and chalk marker. Sew precisely over the line.

Prepare for Quilting

You will need:

- Pieced and Pressed Backing Fabric at least 2-3" larger on all sides than the quilt top
- Low-Loft Batting
- Sulky KK 2000 Temporary Spray Adhesive
- Painter's Masking Tape or Bull Clips
- Rustproof 1" safety pins

Trim off the excess leaving a 1/4" seam allowance. Press the seam open.

Use painter's masking tape to tape the backing fabric (right side down) to a table top or a hard surfaced floor. Keep it taut and smooth without stretching it. Spray half of it with KK 2000. Fold the batting in half and lay it over the sprayed half of the backing fabric. Smooth. Spray the other half of the backing fabric, then smooth out remaining half of batting. Spray the wrong side of the pressed quilt top and smooth over batting. (See photos page 160.)

When using KK 2000, use only half as many pins as you normally would.

Festive, fun theme Quilts with blocks combined from the Sampler Quilt

Snowmen

Taken from the original pattern "Pieces to Quilt" by Marilyn Fisher. Pieced and Quilted by Patsy Shields.

Combined blocks: Rail Fence, My Sulky Star, Crossroads Variation, Benjamin's Kite, and Hole in the Barn Door.

Quilted with Sulky Sliver Metallic Thread #8007 using the Mitten Design (found on pull-out pattern sheet). Sulky Clear Polyester Invisible Thread was used in the bobbin.

Patsy traced the Mitten Design onto Sulky Super Solvy, then sprayed the quilt top with KK 2000 Temporary Spray Adhesive to hold the Mitten design in place while straight stitching over it.

K.P. Kids Fabric Collection by South Seas Imports.

Modeled by Amber Drexler.

Suzy Loves Sulky Frogs

Taken from the original pattern "Pieces to Quilt" by Marilyn Fisher

Suzy Seed
A Sulky National Educator

Suzy's Story about her first attempt at piecing a quilt.

"Oh goody, a box from Sulky. I open it fast and look inside - a pattern and fabric, FROG fabric in red, purple (my favorite colors), green and blue, oh boy, what fun! Then I look at the pattern....IT'S A QUILT PATTERN! WHAT? ...WHO ME? ...Does she have the wrong person? Panic sets in. I don't quilt --- have never even thought I wanted to make a quilt, but the frog fabric is so cute and the creative part of my brain says....'you can do this'.

I made squares??? using all of the fabric sent (all prints). This was not so great. My ASG neighborhood group helped me with placement -- with me insisting that I use every fabric at least once. I learned a lot on those first quilt blocks. 1. Every machine has a different 1/4" foot! 2. I cut very exact and sew less exact because of using different machines. One must be very exact for patterns to mesh. Coming from a garment construction background where there is always room to cheat -- this was a wake-up call. Compound this with the fact I am making this quilt for Joyce Drexler, the 'ULTIMATE' perfectionist, and the stress builds.

I whined and carried on saying over and over 'it's not good enough'. The first set of blocks was horrid. Even I hated them. You just can't use all of those prints and no solids.

Then, wonder of wonders, the second set of blocks was so cute I almost hoped Joyce wouldn't like it. Then it could be mine.

This was a wonderful growing experience in my sewing career, and I now thank Joyce for the opportunity to make a quilt top for her. I will do another quilt one day, as a matter of fact, I have fabric for 2 already."

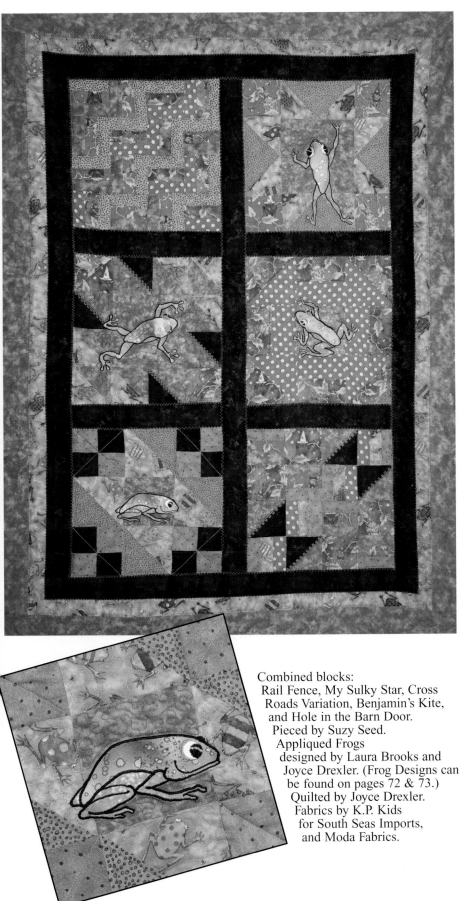

Combined blocks:
Rail Fence, My Sulky Star, Cross Roads Variation, Benjamin's Kite, and Hole in the Barn Door.
Pieced by Suzy Seed.
Appliqued Frogs designed by Laura Brooks and Joyce Drexler. (Frog Designs can be found on pages 72 & 73.)
Quilted by Joyce Drexler.
Fabrics by K.P. Kids for South Seas Imports, and Moda Fabrics.

SWIRL DESIGN:
(see Quilt Block on page 9).
Trace onto Sulky Solvy.

FROG DESIGN:
(see Quilt on page 71) has
been reversed for easy
tracing onto paper-backed
fusible web.

CRANE DESIGN:
(see Quilt on page 25).
Trace onto Sulky Solvy.

ROSE SWIRL DESIGN:
(see Quilt on Back Cover).
Trace onto Sulky Solvy.

72

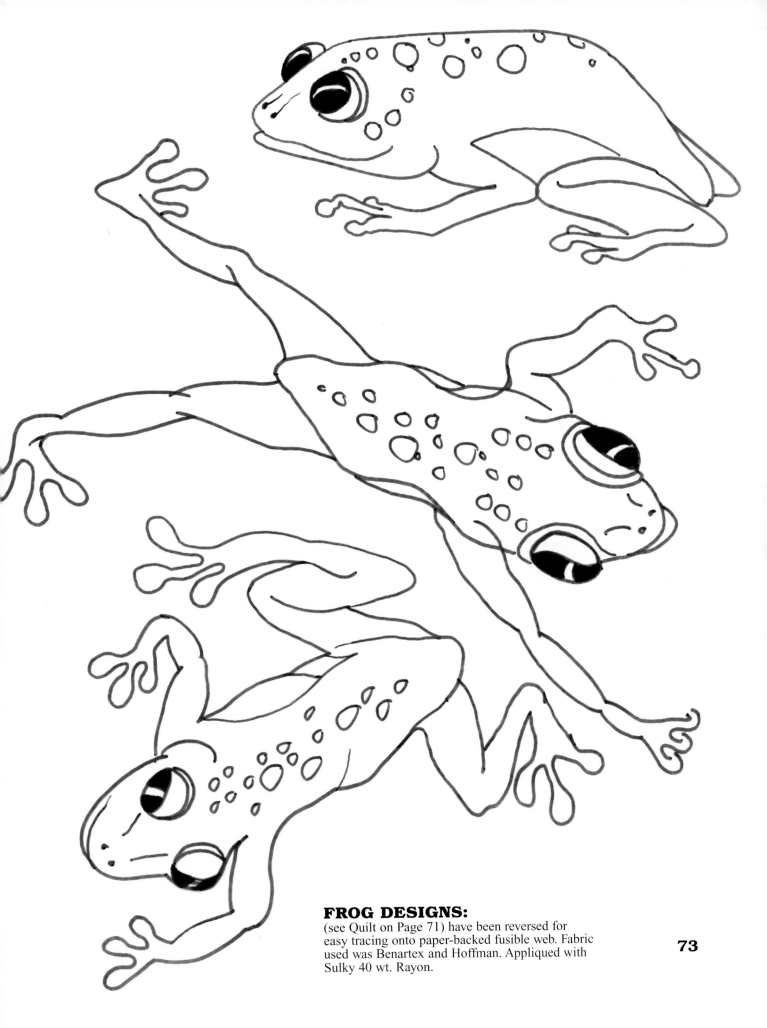

FROG DESIGNS:
(see Quilt on Page 71) have been reversed for
easy tracing onto paper-backed fusible web. Fabric
used was Benartex and Hoffman. Appliqued with
Sulky 40 wt. Rayon.

73

I've Fallen for Sulky

Featuring Computerized Machine Embroidery stitched with Amazing Designs AD#1013 Spring Holiday Collection I.

Embroidered by Evelyn Howard on the Esante'. Pieced and Quilted by Joyce Drexler.

A variation of the Cross Roads Variation in which Quarter-Square Triangle Squares were substituted for Half-Square Triangle Squares.

Echo and Stipple Quilted with 2 strands of 35 wt. Sulky Ultra Twist #3009 in the needle and Sulky #3009 in the Bobbin.

Fabrics: M & M Fabrics by South Seas Imports.

74

In this quilt, we have alternated the center square of each block with a fussy cut "Love" fabric and the Embroidered Cupid using selected Sulky colors that matched the little Cupids in the fabric print. When picking Sulky Colors for your embroidery, you don't always have to follow the suggested colors given with the card. Choose from the 337 colors of Sulky 40 wt. Rayon that best blend with your fabric selection.

Marilyn Fisher

Sulky National
Educator & Designer
from Holland, MI

Marilyn has sewn for as long as she can remember. Her Mother was a seamstress and taught the girls to sew, usually using feed sacks for the projects.

Marilyn graduated from Western Michigan University with a B.S. & M.A. in Teaching of Home Economics, Textiles & Art. She has taught in 4 Michigan High Schools and has been teaching some aspect of sewing for the past 30 years, and teaching quilting for about 20 years.

For 12 years she and her late husband, Walt, owned a Fabric and Sewing Machine Store. She designed the "Pieces to Quilt" patterns for Speed Stitch, Inc., and has written many articles for Arts and Crafts Magazines.

Marilyn specializes in Machine Arts and Quilting and has taught many classes throughout the United States. She has taught at conventions such as "SMART", IN STITCHES, NQA, and QUILT MARKET and she is a NATIONAL EDUCATOR FOR SULKY OF AMERICA, teaching Sulky "Sew Exciting" Seminars.

She is a member of West Michigan Quilt Guild, A Quilt Study Group, Michigan Quilt Network, NQA, NQSG, AQS and a Friendship Quilter's Bee.

She has 4 children, and 5 grandchildren, all of which she is very proud. For relaxation she works in her English Garden, loves to travel, designs and pieces quilts, and organizes and teaches "Quilter's Retreat" Weekends. Her greatest joys are seeing the happiness when someone receives one of her quilts, and the satisfaction students receive from completing a project she has taught.

"Oh Holy Night"

"O Holy Night" has always been a favorite Christmas Carol. The music was written by the French composer Adolphe Charles Adam. At the time he composed the music it was frowned on by church authorities and the church denounced it for its "lack of musical taste and total absence of the spirit of religion" according to one French bishop. The English words we use today were written by an American clergyman and musical authority named John Sullivan Dwight. It has become one of the most popular Christmas solos today. (Information from The Reader's Digest Merry Christmas Songbook.)

The first project of the Christmas Quartet is the mini-sampler Bell Pull. The blocks were chosen to represent that First Holy Night: The Spinning Star, Hole in the Barn Door and Lady of the Lake. One block of each is used in this project. The Stocking also has 3 blocks. The Table Runner has 7 blocks: 2 each of Lady of the Lake and Hole in the Barn Door, and 3 Star blocks. The wall hanging has 9 blocks of 3 each. All projects are set on the diagonal.

✂ Cutting Guide for Bell Pull

- 3/4 yd. Main Print for blocks, 2nd border (cut 3-1/2" wide) and binding (cut 2-1/2" wide)
- 1/2 yd. Light Background Fabric for blocks
- 1/4 yd. Medium Color Fabric for sides and corners.
- 1/8 yd. Contrast Accent color for 1st border (cut 1-1/2" wide)
- 1/2 yd. Solid or Print for backing
- 15" x 30" piece of Batting
- Cut six 2" squares of Background Fabric.
- Cut two 2" squares of Main Fabric.
- Cut one 1-1/4" x 9" strip each from Main Fabric and Background Fabric and sew them together using a scant 1/4" seam. Cut into four 2" squares.
- From the <u>medium color</u> fabric cut one 8-1/2" square. RECUT this square into quarters <u>diagonally</u> from corner to corner to make 4 triangles for the side.
- From the <u>medium color</u> fabric cut one 4-1/2" square. RECUT this square in half diagonally to make 2 triangles for 2 top corners.
- To make your half-square triangles cut one 10-1/2" x 15" piece each of Main Print and Background Fabric.

2

Basic Construction Directions

Sew each block individually. Use a scant 1/4" seam allowance throughout blockmaking, assembling and finishing. Refer to directions in the Sampler Quilt for the blocks, Hole in the Barn Door (p. 38) and Spinning Star (p. 34). The Lady of the Lake is not in the Sampler Quilt - see layout on the left.

Instructions for Blocks:

1. Use 1-1/2" Finished Triangle Paper and the 10-1/2" x 15" piece of main print and background fabric (as directed on page 34) to make the triangles. Trim off corners.

2. Using photos as your guide, sew pieces together to make rows.

3. Sew rows together. Press seams, usually to the print side.

Note: "The Lady of the Lake Block" is very simple. Arrange the 7 half-square triangles as shown with one Background Fabric square in the upper right hand corner, and one Main Fabric square in the lower left hand corner.

ASSEMBLING:

1. Using the 4 large triangles (for the sides) and 2 small triangles (for the top corners), lay out blocks and contrast triangles.

2. Sew blocks, side, and top triangles together in rows diagonally. All triangles will have straight of grain on the outside. Press.

   Note: Some of the side and top triangles may not be even on the outside, so trim off all excess, leaving a 1/4" seam allowance.

3. Add sides, top and bottom of 1st Border. Press.

4. Add sides, top and bottom of 2nd Border. Press.

 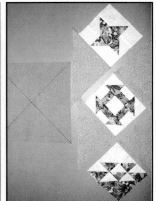

FINISHING:
(See Finishing Instructions on pages 157-160.)

1. Layer backing, batting and top together using Sulky KK-2000 and a few very small safety pins (if needed).

2. Machine quilt as desired, using Sulky Sliver #8040 Opalescent Thread. (Marilyn did *Stipple Quilting*.)

3. Trim excess batting and backing.

4. Using a 1/4" seam allowance, sew on 2-1/2" wide French Fold binding strips that are folded in half and pressed; fold to the back and sew down by hand.

✄ Cutting Guide for Other Projects

The other three parts of this quartet are constructed in the same manner; just more yardage is needed.

For the Table Runner, cut three 8-1/2" squares. You will need 12 side triangles and no corners. Also make 3 Star Blocks and 2 each of the other two Blocks.

For the Wall Hanging, cut two 8-1/2" squares and two 4-1/2" squares. You will need 8 triangles and 4 corners. Make 3 each of the 3 Blocks.

For the Stocking, make the Bell Pull and simply add the toe of the stocking from the background fabric.

77

"I like using ALL of the Sulky products because they make my creative projects go together quickly and efficiently, thereby saving me time.

Sulky's wide range of thread colors is fantastic. I find Sulky products are consistently high quality and easy to use.

Finding the right shades for the flowers was an important aspect of this project. Sulky's large color selection afforded me the opportunity to select colors that complemented each other while creating the illusion of depth.

The vibrant sheens assured me that the flowers would be an eye-catcher."
--- Sharon

Fabric credits: P & B white-on-white fabric was used for the background of the flowers. A light green RJR fabric was used for the pineapple strips and corner fabric. The medium green pineapple strip is a Benartex fabric and the dark green strip is a Moda print.

78

**Sharon Stokes & Pumpkin
Franklin, NC**

Sharon and her husband, John, live halfway up Nickajack Mountain in Franklin, NC. She is the principal in Sharon's Quilt Shoppe, a major part of their Carolina Sew & Vac store, which is an authorized Janome and Singer Sewing Machine Dealer.

Sharon is a designer and a teacher. In 1976, it was Joyce Drexler who introduced Sharon to the creativity of free-motion machine embroidery. In 1977, she began her professional sewing career by teaching free-motion embroidery, clothing construction, applique, and other classes. While teaching for six years, she and John began a cottage business designing and making customized free-motion embroidered and appliqued clothing and household items.

In 1983, she and John purchased Peace River Sew & Vac in Arcadia, FL and Sharon began shifting the store to a quilting operation. In 1990, they moved their home and business to Franklin, NC. She has served two terms as president of the Smoky Mountain Quilt Guild.

Since 1983, she has attended the International Quilt Market in Houston each year, taking classes from highly recognized designers and quilters such as Jinny Beyer, Eleanor Burns, Harriet Hargrave, Elly Sienkiewicz and others. Through all this, she has been a homemaker and raised two children, John Jr. and Cheryl.

Cheryl tells everyone "Pumpkin is the third child". John and Sharon call her their "little person" since she is a very intelligent and loving cat. Sharon says, "She came to our home one day in January and would not leave; after about a week she convinced us she was going to be our cat. That was eleven years ago!

Pumpkin oversees the household and sees that we do things right. She has her own quilt next to the sewing machine so she can be readily available for her sewing input when she thinks it's needed. Occasionally she prefers to assist with the sewing, and picks a spot to lay right in front of the sewing machine in order to provide close personal attention. She has a 'paw' in everything I sew!"

Pineapples in my Flower Garden

*Designed & Quilted
by Sharon Stokes*

*Using Pineapple
Foundation Piecing Papers
from Lynn Graves*

✂ Cutting Guide

**Always cut the selvages off the fabric
before cutting strips.**

✂ 1 yd. of 45" background fabric for flowers

✂ 1 yd. each of 45" medium and dark fabric for pineapple strips and borders

✂ 1 yd. of 45" light fabric for pineapple strips and corners

**Pineapple
Foundation Sheets**
available from:
*Carolina Sew & Vac
39 Palmer St. Circle
Franklin, NC 28734
(828) 524-3046*

SUPPLIES:

• Sulky 40 wt. Rayon Thread in assorted floral colors
• Sulky Polyester Bobbin Thread
• Sulky Invisible Polyester Thread
• 1 pkg. of Sulky Totally Stable Iron-On Stabilizer
• 1 pkg. of Sulky Tear-Easy Stabilizer
• Sulky KK 2000 Temporary Spray Adhesive
• 1 pkg. of Sulky Solvy Stabilizer
• Lynn Graves' Pineapple Foundation Sheets
• Continuous Line "Leaping Leaves" Design by Hari Walner (See pull-out pattern sheet.)

EMBROIDERY CARDS USED:

• Singer XL 1000's Built-In Floral Designs
• Singer Gigantic Floral #15
• Singer Large Flowers #IV

79

PREPARE FABRIC FOR COMPUTERIZED MACHINE EMBROIDERY:

1. Cut nine 9" x 14" pieces out of the background fabric to fit the large machine embroidery hoop.

2. Iron Totally Stable onto the back of all 9 pieces, then hoop the first one. Use KK 2000 to temporarily adhere two layers of Tear-Easy together, then adhere the two-layer sandwich to the bottom of the hooped fabric, again using KK 2000.

3. After embroidering a floral design with Sulky 40 wt. Rayon colors, remove it from the hoop and tear away the Tear-Easy one layer at a time; then remove the Totally Stable. Repeat for the other 8 pieces, using either the same floral design, different designs, or a combination you choose.

PREPARE EMBROIDERED PIECE FOR FOUNDATION PIECING:

1. Cut each block down to 6-1/2" square. Lightly spray the back of the square with KK 2000.

2. Place the square on top of the Pineapple Foundation Sheet so the fabric is in the middle of the paper. Follow the directions for foundation piecing found in package.

PIECE QUILT TOP:

1. After completing all 9 blocks, leave foundation paper on and sew them together in a manner that pleases you.

2. After the blocks have been sewn together, remove the foundation paper from the back.

3. Cut inside border 2-1/2" and outside border 3-1/2"; sew them onto the quilt with a 1/4" seam allowance.

4. After sewing the borders to the quilt, miter the corners.

PREPARE TO QUILT:

1. To prepare the borders for quilting, draw or trace a design onto Sulky Solvy, then lightly spray the back of it with KK 2000 and place it on the borders. Free-motion quilt over the design. To remove Solvy quickly and easily, wet a Q-tip and run it along the stitching line. The Solvy comes away perfectly without making the quilt wet. Bind the edges. (Quilt design on pattern sheet).

Bears 'N Paws

Designed, Pieced and Quilted by Sharon Stokes

1 ✂ Cutting Guide

**Always cut the selvages off the fabric
before cutting strips.**

- ✂ 1-1/2 yards Sulky Totally Stable Iron-on Stabilizer
- ✂ 1-1/2 yards Sulky Super Solvy Water Soluble Stabilizer
- ✂ 1 yard of P & B Naturescape Bear Fabric
  for sixteen 4-1/2" Bear Squares
  and 1-1/3 yards for back of quilt
- ✂ 1-1/4 yards Dark fabric for half-square
  triangles, sashing and narrow border
- ✂ 1-1/2 yards Light fabric for half-square
  triangles, sashing and wide borders
- ✂ 1/3 yard Fabric for Binding
- ✂ 1-1/3 yards Batting

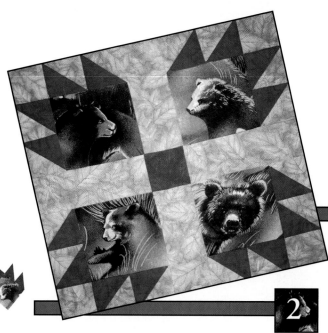

SUPPLIES:

- Sulky 40 wt. Rayon Thread
- Sulky Smoke Invisible Polyester Thread
- Sulky KK 2000 Temporary Spray Adhesive
- 2" Half-Square Triangle paper (3 sheets)
- Safety Pins for Basting
- Good Quality Sewing Thread
- 75/11 Quilting Needle & 90/14 Needle
- Rotary Cutter, Mat and Ruler

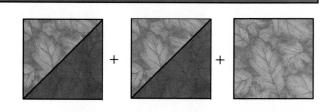

MAKING THE BLOCKS:

1. Cut two 10" x 16" pieces of fabric, 1 light and 1 dark. Lightly spray KK 2000 onto the right side of the dark piece of fabric and place the light piece of fabric on top of it, right sides together. Lightly spray KK 2000 onto the wrong side of the top fabric and place the 2" half-square triangle paper on top of it. You now have a nice sandwich that will stay together without pinning while you sew. With regular sewing thread, straight stitch on the dotted lines with a short stitch length and a size 90/14 needle to make the paper tear away more easily. Using the same procedure, sew the other two sheets together. Use your ruler and rotary cutter to cut the half-squares apart on the **solid** line. Press open with the seam toward the dark fabric. Gently tear away the triangle paper. Make 64 of these half-square triangles.

2. "Fussy cut" (see page 48) sixteen 4-1/2" squares that each include a bear from the bear fabric. Use a clear ruler so you can see the bears as you cut out each one.

3. From the light fabric, cut sixteen 2-1/2" x 6-1/2" strips and seventeen 2-1/2" squares. From the dark fabric, cut four 2-1/2" x 14-1/2" strips and four 2-1/2" squares.

4. Rotate the individual half-square triangles so that they will face in the right direction to complete each Bear Paw Block. Refer to photo above for correct placement.

5. Join two half-square triangle squares together, again referring to picture for proper direction.

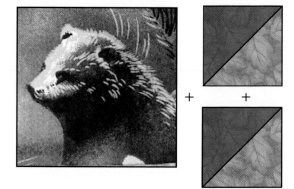

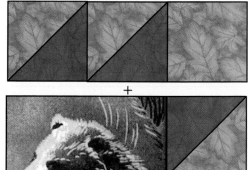

6. When sewing the 4-1/2" Bear Print to the bottom two squares of each block, check the direction and placement of the Bear's head to be sure it will be facing the desired direction. Join one 2-1/2" solid light square to the two toe squares. Check picture for proper placement.

7. Sew the pieces to the 4-1/2" square in the sequence needed to complete the Bear Paw Block, again referring to the picture. All together, 16 blocks will be required: four of each Bear Paw according to the placement of the toe squares.

8. Sew a finished Bear square to a light 2-1/2" x 6-1/2" strip. Add another finished Bear square to the other side of the 6-1/2" strip. Repeat procedure for the bottom two squares.

9. Join top and bottom squares together by sewing a sashing made of two light 2-1/2" x 6-1/2" strips with a dark 2-1/2" square in between the light strips.

10. Join the two finished top squares vertically, using the dark 2-1/2" x 14-1/2" strip to join them. Do the same with the two bottom squares with a 2-1/2" x 14-1/2" strip. Join the remaining two 2-1/2" x 14-1/2" strips together with the light 2-1/2" square in the middle. Use this strip to join the two top completed squares to the bottom two completed squares.

NARROW ACCENT BORDER AND WIDE BORDER:

Cut two 2-1/2" x 30-1/2" dark strips and sew them onto each side. Cut two 2-1/2" x 34-1/2" dark strips and sew them to the top and bottom.

Cut 2 light strips 3-1/2" x 34-1/2" and sew to each side. Cut 2 light strips 3-1/2" x 40-1/2" and sew to top and bottom.

LAYER, QUILT, BIND:

1. Lay the backing down first with the wrong side up and spray it with KK 2000. Lay the batting over the backing. Spray the wrong side of the quilt top with KK 2000 and place it over the batting. You now have a secure sandwich that will require about half as many pins to baste.

2. Quilt using your favorite method. Sharon drew large and small bear silhouettes (one for each border) and traced them onto a strip of Totally Stable the same width and length of each border, which made it easy for her to get proper placement of the bears on the Totally Stable. She cut away the inside of the bears on the traced lines, leaving bear silhouettes which she ironed onto the borders. She then free-motion stitched around the inside of each "empty" bear using Sulky Smoke Polyester Invisible Thread. This way there was no stabilizer to tear or dissolve away from stitching. Clever! Sharon then traced oak leaves onto Sulky Solvy, adhered the Solvy to the sashing with KK 2000, and free-motion quilted the leaves with Sulky 40 wt. Rayon #1035 on the red fabric and Sulky 40 wt. Rayon #1266 on the tan fabric. To remove the Solvy without washing the quilt, wet a Q-Tip and run it over the quilting stitches to dissolve the Solvy so it pulls away easily.

3. Bind (see General Finishing Instructions on pages 69 and 157-160).

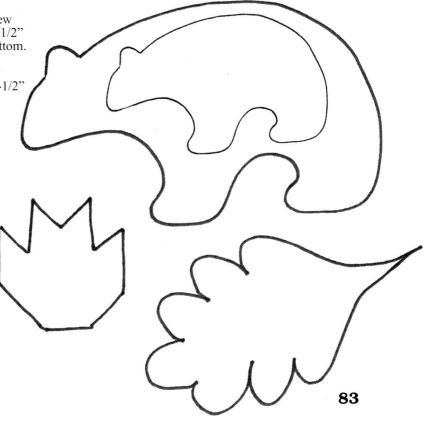

83

Laura Ashley™ Paws

Designed and Pieced by Joyce Drexler
Quilted by Tina Ignatowicz

Joyce needed a king-size bed cover for the bed in the master bedroom of her North Carolina Summer Home. Rather than using only quilting fabrics, she elected to take a sheet and curtain from the Laura Ashley Collection that she used in the bed linens, towels and curtains so that it would all coordinate. Quilted on a long-arm professional machine using Sulky 30 wt. Rayon Threads, Off White #1071, Teal #1046 and Med. Burgundy #1190.

84

Camouflage Cats - Finished Size: 71" x 90"

Trish Liden (with husband Ray)
National Sulky Educator
Camarillo, CA

Creative stitching and Textile Art are an integral part of Trish's background. She earned a Bachelor's Degree in Home Economics with an emphasis on Clothing/Textiles/Art. She attends continuing education classes to maintain her status as a Certified Home Economist and enthusiastically welcomes opportunities to learn from others in the industry.

Prior to becoming a National Sulky Educator, Trish taught at a well-established sewing machine dealership and fabric/quilt shop in Southern California. She has been a four-term officer of her local Quilt Guild.

She loves to pass her enthusiasm for "exploration" of fabric and art to her students to inspire "the artist within". Trish believes that stitching enthusiasts are some of the most friendly, sharing people in the world. It is her pleasure to meet with them and to teach (and learn from) those who share her love of creative sewing.

Camouflage Cats

Designed, Pieced and Quilted by Trish Liden
Shown by Joyce Drexler on the PBS TV Show
KAYE'S QUILTING FRIENDS

"Staggered Bargello Piecing"

"Camouflage Cats was created as a Christmas gift for my husband, Ray, an avid outdoorsman. It was my goal to combine animal prints into a modern design and to incorporate a variety of Sulky threads and techniques into the quilt. The basic design was based on the Staggered Bargello Technique used in the Sulky 'Sew Exciting' Seminar II Vest Project which I teach." --- Trish

✂ Cutting Guide
Always cut the selvages off the fabric before cutting strips.

Select fabrics that grade in color, have a variety of interest in print, and will carry the theme. You could combine two to six large blocks (each approximately 17" square, finished) to make a small wallhanging or a full size quilt. Fabric amounts below are for a full size quilt with 6 blocks.

You will arrange fabrics in a pleasing manner, example: gold to rust, grey to black, etc.

✂ 1/4 yard each of 10-15 assorted animal prints
✂ 1/4 yard each of 10-15 cotton prints that "set off" the featured animal prints
✂ 2/3 yd. Zebra print for sashing and inner border
✂ Approx. 4 yds. charcoal/black fabric for sashing and binding
✂ Batting - Queen Size
✂ 4-1/2 yds. fabric for backing

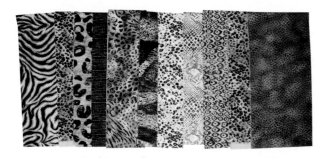

MAKE THE STRIP SETS

1. For each strip set, cut a 45" long strip from each fabric. Cut widths that vary from 1-1/2" to 3-1/2" wide (example: 1-1/2", 2", 2-1/4", 3-1/4" etc.), except for the first and last pieces which must be at least 5" wide.

Fabric Credits: P & B Fabrics, South Seas Imports, Hi-Fashion Fabrics, RJR Fabrics, Hoffman Fabrics and Moda Fabrics.

"Bridges"

2. Using a 1/4" seam allowance, stitch each set of strips together to make a strata. Press seams in one direction.

3. Slice the first part of the strata vertically into pieces 2" to 4" wide, varying the widths as in #1, to make approximately 8 to 12 strips. When stitched together later using a 1/4" seam allowance, the finished width needs to be approximately 16"-18" wide.

4. Cut the rest of the strata into 4" strips (for the animal border). Set aside.

STITCH THE BARGELLO BLOCKS:

1. Lay out the strips shifting them up and down in a staggered pattern. When you are pleased with the layout, trim off the uneven edges of the top and bottom.

2. Choose a wider strip (3" to 4") in an area where you want to feature the animal eyes or faces. Unsew this piece from the strip with your seam ripper.

3. Select an area to "feature" (note animal eyes). Remove this piece of fabric and use it as a template to cut the "featured" detail. Stitch the "surprise" fabric in place of the original fabric.

4. Sew these strips together lengthwise with the top ends flush. Always make sure the #2 color is on the top end of the strip. The bottom ends may not necessarily be flush.

Do not try to match the seams. This is a fast and easy method. Press seams in one direction.

REPEAT ABOVE PROCESS FOR THE REST OF THE THEME BLOCKS.

5. Trim all blocks to the same measurement, approximately 17" x 17", or to whatever size the smallest block measures.

CUT SASHING:

Cut these Sashing Strips from mottled charcoal/black fabric to set off the blocks: *Note: Length is approximate and will be determined by your block measurement.*

- Three 4" x 17" sashing strips to place between two-block sets vertically.
- Six 8" x 17" Sashing Strips to place vertically at each side of the two-block sets.
- Two 4" x 54" Sashing Strips to place horizontally between the two-block sets.
- Two 8" x 54" Sashing Strips to place horizontally at top and bottom of blocks.

LAYER & QUILT:

Layer backing fabric, batting and quilt top.
Pin together for the quilting process. Time to play
with thread and stitch variations:

1. Using Sulky Invisible Smoke Thread, stitch "in
   the ditch" (see page 10) around the theme
   blocks and animal print border.

2. Using Sulky Sliver #8011 Light Copper and a
   straight stitch setting, free-motion (see page 55)
   stitch a swirl design over the theme blocks to
   soften the geometric lines of the blocks.

3. Across the quilt, stitch a soft wave design with
   either a free-motion or a machine-fed straight
   stitch.

4. Using a number of colors and types of Sulky
   Threads, straight stitch random geometric
   patterns across the animal print border.

5. Add Confetti:
   To make Confetti, tie off, satin stitch approximately 1+ inch, then tie off again.
   Vary the Confetti widths and lengths while
   scattering a variety of Sulky Sliver Metallic and
   Rayon Threads (that coordinate with the animal
   prints) all over the entire quilt.

6. Bind the quilt using zebra printed fabric.
   Sign quilt. Enjoy.

88

SASHING & BRIDGES:

1. Build "Bridges" of colored fabric and Sashing
   Fabric. Use more colors of fabric, some leftover pieces and interesting textures, etc. Stitch
   1/4" seam allowances and splice the "Bridges"
   into the Sashing at the appropriate places.

2. Stitch Sashing to top and bottom of Blocks.
   Join the vertical Sashing units to the sides and
   center of the Theme Blocks.

3. For the Animal Sashing, clip open the rest of
   the 4" Sashing Sets and stitch them to form a
   continuous blend of all of the theme prints.
   Large pieces of fabric (first and last in each set)
   will need to be narrowed.

ZEBRA STRIP & STRATA:

To the outside sashing, stitch a strip of 1-1/2"
wide zebra fabric. Stitch the multi-colored
animal strata to the zebra sashing. Finish with
a 4-6" strip of charcoal/black mottled Sashing.

Bear Clan Totem Pole Vest

Designed, Appliqued and Quilted
by Sharon Boysen

Fabric Credit:
Timeless Treasure Collection
by Hi-Fashion Fabrics

To order the vest pattern
contact: The Berry Patch
15N 270 Sleepy Hollow Road
Sleepy Hollow, IL 60118

The Totem Pole is a very important part of the culture of the Indians in the Pacific Northwest. This Totem Pole honors the Bear, a very strong and powerful animal. The bottom Bear is reared up in a guard position. Sitting above him is yet another Bear on watch. At the very top of the Totem Pole perches the all-seeing Raven. Each seems more watchful when embellished with the double button eyes. And, no, they do not hurt when you wear the vest! You'll be able to see where you've been!

Sharon Boysen
Designer from Sleepy Hollow, IL

Sharon lives on what could best be described as a sunny, woody lot. With the best of both types of gardening available, the yard keeps her outdoors in the dirt most of the growing season. Her three German Shepards (Zeus, Juno & Sheba - all littermates) enjoy any time spent in the garden. Inspiration for some of her patterns have come from the flowers and plants growing there. In 1995, she established a pattern company, Designs from the Berry Patch, in response to requests for patterns for the vests she wore.

A mother of four and a proud grandmother of seven (soon to be nine), she has plenty of willing models for the garments she designs. With years of working with children in a library and school environment, she developed an interest in the many cultures of the Native American people. According to Sharon, when she first saw the fabric used for the Bear Totem Vest, it just called to her for a Totem Pole. A love of buttons, especially to embellish a design, and the love of fabrics have been a part of her life since childhood.

90

1

VEST:
- Vest Pattern of your choice. Sharon used her own pattern #DBPO12.
- 1-1/4 yds. each of Vest Fabric, lining fabric and flannel for interlining
- 3 buttons (JHB #80543 - Totem Pole)
- Thread for construction

DESIGN:
- 1 Fat Quarter each of four colors for the Bear Fetish and Totem Pole Designs
- Sulky 30 wt. Rayon Threads to match four colors above
- Sulky 30 wt. Rayon Thread to topstitch vest
- Sulky Bobbin Thread
- Sulky KK 2000 Temporary Spray Adhesive
- Sulky Tear-Easy and Totally Stable Stabilizers
- Buttons & Beads for embellishing the design: 8 to 10 JHB #42650 1/2" white shirt buttons, 12 to 14 JHB #47376 1/8" black Barbie buttons, 4 JHB #70314 pearl bird-shaped buttons, beads for embellishment of Bear Fetish - *optional*

Note: Prewash all fabrics to avoid disappointments due to colors running or fabric shrinkage.

2

PREPARE TO APPLIQUE:

Using a vest pattern of your choice, spray it with Sulky KK-2000 to hold the pattern in place while you cut out the vest, lining and interlining. Press all pieces. Use a light spray of KK 2000 to temporarily "tack" the vest fabric pieces onto the flannel interlining.

Trace all of the design elements from pages 92 and 93 onto Totally Stable. Rough-cut the Totally Stable pattern and iron it onto the appropriate fabric, or trace onto any paper and use KK 2000 to hold it in place while tracing and cutting. Use the pattern pieces to cut out the Bear Clan Totem Pole and the Bear Fetishes from the design fabrics; also prepare a Totem Pole for the lining back of the vest to add a bit of surprise in the garment. Lightly spray the wrong side of the design fabric pieces with KK 2000.

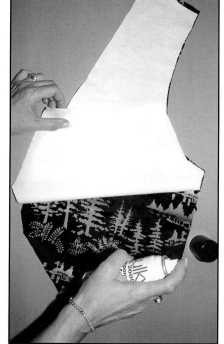

(If you want to fuse them permanently, use a fusible web.) Center the Totem Pole Pieces on the vest back. When placing the Totem Pole on the lining, to stabilize it, spray KK 2000 on a piece of Tear-Easy and place it on the wrong side of the lining.

To give more of a hand-done look, lengthen the width and length of a Blanket Stitch or a Zig-Zag Stitch, and outline the design through both layers of fabric. To make a heavier look to your stitch, use either Sulky 30 wt., two strands of 40 wt., or Sulky 35 wt. Ultra Twist. Use Sulky Bobbin Thread in the bobbin and lower the top tension slightly so the Bobbin Thread does not show.

3

BEADS & BUTTONS EMBELLISHMENTS:

If you have decided to add the "surprise" on the lining back, take parts of the Totem Pole design and create your own Totem Pole surprise; embellish with stitching and buttons.

The Bear Fetishes may be embellished with the Mountain Design and the Bird on its shoulder. An interesting option would be to "tie" the Bird onto the Bear with a string of small beads. As you hand sew the "string" in place, be sure to secure the beads every three or four beads by taking a stitch into the Bear Fabric. Make frequent knots as you work to secure the beads. Don't forget to give the Bear an eye so he can see his way. The tiny black button (#47376) gives the Bear a very shiny black eye.

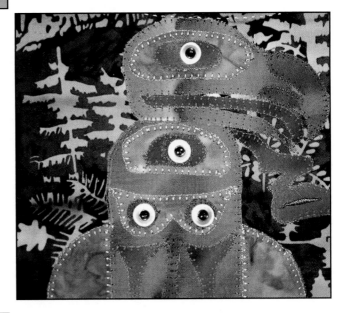

4

ASSEMBLE THE VEST:

Assemble the Vest and its lining according to the Vest pattern directions. Press well. Use either Sulky 30 wt. Rayon or 35 wt. Ultra Twist to add top-stitching either by hand or by machine. You may want to finish off the shoulders with fabric triangles in a row along the seam line, using the same fabric used in the totem poles and the bear fetishes. Stitch through all layers of fabrics and see what you want to add to the look.

Using a 30 wt. Sulky Rayon, Sharon hand-quilted a topstitch about 3/8" from all edges.

Try using this "Design from the Berry Patch" on a sweatshirt or a ready-made garment.

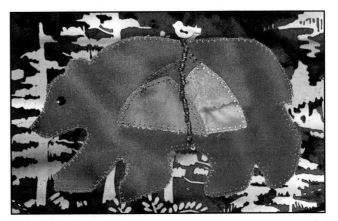

91

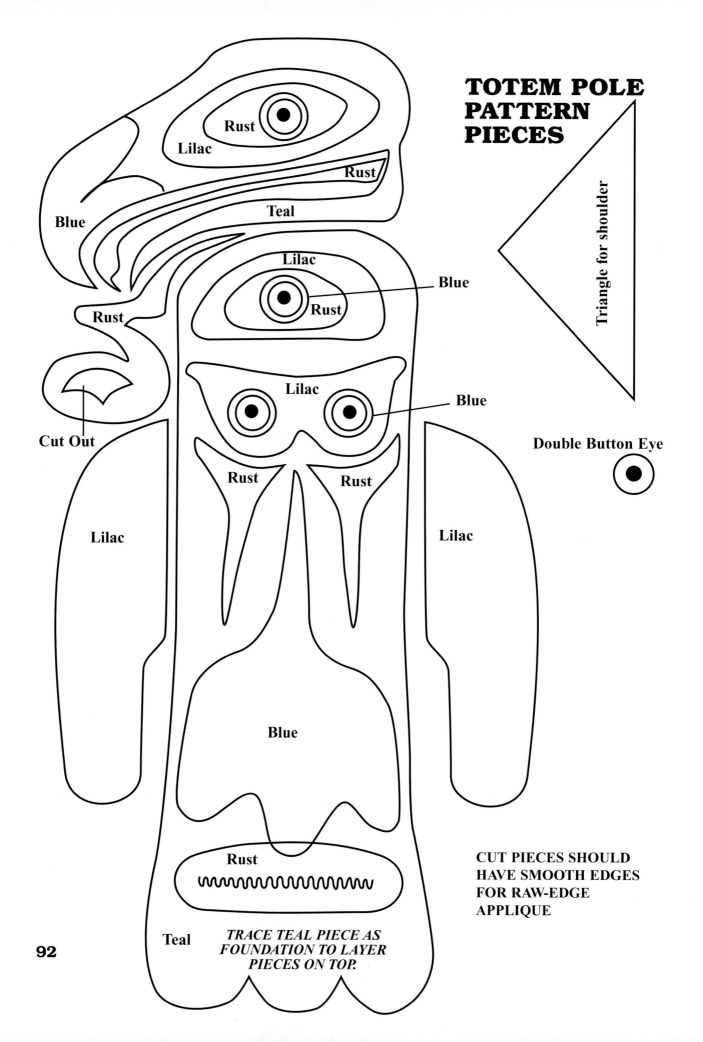

TOTEM POLE PATTERN PIECES

Rust

Lilac

Rust

Teal

Blue

Lilac

Blue

Rust

Rust

Lilac

Cut Out

Blue

Rust

Rust

Lilac

Lilac

Blue

Rust

Teal

Triangle for shoulder

Double Button Eye

CUT PIECES SHOULD HAVE SMOOTH EDGES FOR RAW-EDGE APPLIQUE

TRACE TEAL PIECE AS FOUNDATION TO LAYER PIECES ON TOP.

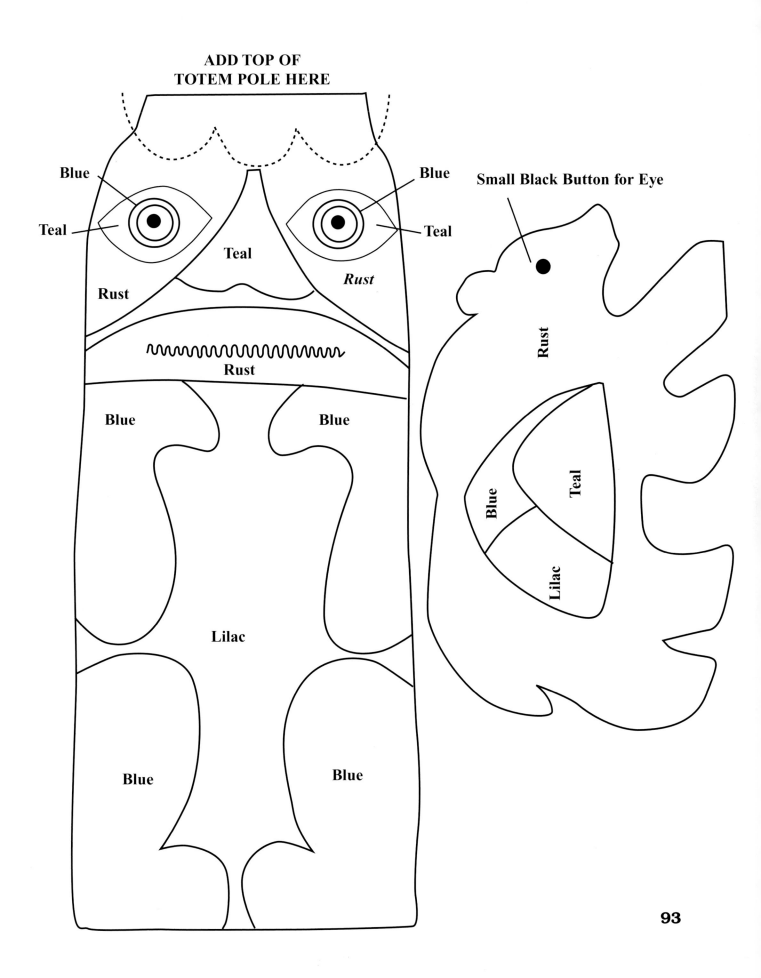

**ADD TOP OF
TOTEM POLE HERE**

Blue

Teal

Teal

Rust

Rust

Rust

Blue

Blue

Lilac

Blue

Blue

Blue

Teal

Small Black Button for Eye

Rust

Blue

Teal

Lilac

93

Cheri Applegate

Jill Peak & her Mom,
Ethel Springer

Sonya Anderson &
Vicki Schaller

Debbie Carroll
& her stepmother, Patti Lee

Loretta Durian & Joyce Drexler

94

Squares & Rectangles 125" x 125"
Designed and Pieced by Joyce Drexler, Quilted by Donna Agnelly
using Sulky 30 wt. Rayon #1128.

Donna Agnelly
*Quilt Instructor
for Hearthside Quilter's Nook
Hales Corners, WI*

Donna began quilting in 1978. She learned from her Mother and started out strictly hand-quilting before moving into machine work. Her first quilt was a Grandmother's Flower Garden. Her Mom said she had to quilt every hexagon, and she did. She has been teaching for Hearthside Quilters Nook in Hales Corners, WI, for over 13 years. She loves teaching, quilting and working with fabrics and colors.

Donna's daughter, Audra, 21, who is graduating from college, was the inspiration and co-teacher of the Mom-Daughter class at the shop. Her son, Brett, 23, is cognitively disabled - he is a high-functioning autistic and very "special" to her. You might call him her wardrobe consultant (she calls him the "Dictator"). He knows every item of clothing she owns and delights in telling her what to wear and when to wear it. He is her constant ego booster - every quilt she makes is wonderful, according to Brett.

A Scrap Quilt
"Squares & Rectangles"

The Half-Wits' Class has become a bi-annual quilting party organized around Joyce Drexler's and Patti Lee's trips to Milwaukee to tape PBS TV shows. At each class the participants decide what they would like to make at the next class. Sometimes, they actually do two quilt tops in the two days they are together.

✂ Cutting Guide

1

Always cut the selvages off the fabric before cutting strips.

Use those scraps that you've been saving for a rainy day or select 1/2 yd. of 12-15 coordinating fabrics for making the Scrap Blocks. You will need more yardage for Borders, solid Blocks, Backing and Binding.

- ✂ 3-3/4 yards of Darks
- ✂ 3-1/4 yards of Lights
- ✂ 3-3/4 yards for Sashing
- ✂ 3 yards for Border
  (Joyce used a Border Print that gave the effect of triple borders.)
- ✂ 3-1/2 yards for Binding
- ✂ Fairfield Low-Loft Batting
- ✂ 10-1/2 yards for Backing

The majority of fabrics used were from the William Morris Collection. Others used: South Seas Imports, Moda Fabrics and Hoffman Fabrics.

Featuring a Continuous Line Pattern #6113 by Karla Schulz for EZ Quilting by Wrights.

To hold continuous line drawings, like the one used on this quilt, spray Sulky KK 2000 Temporary Spray Adhesive on the underside of the pattern and smooth it onto the fabric for easy quilting of that design without pins. (Border quilting design is also on pull-out pattern sheet).

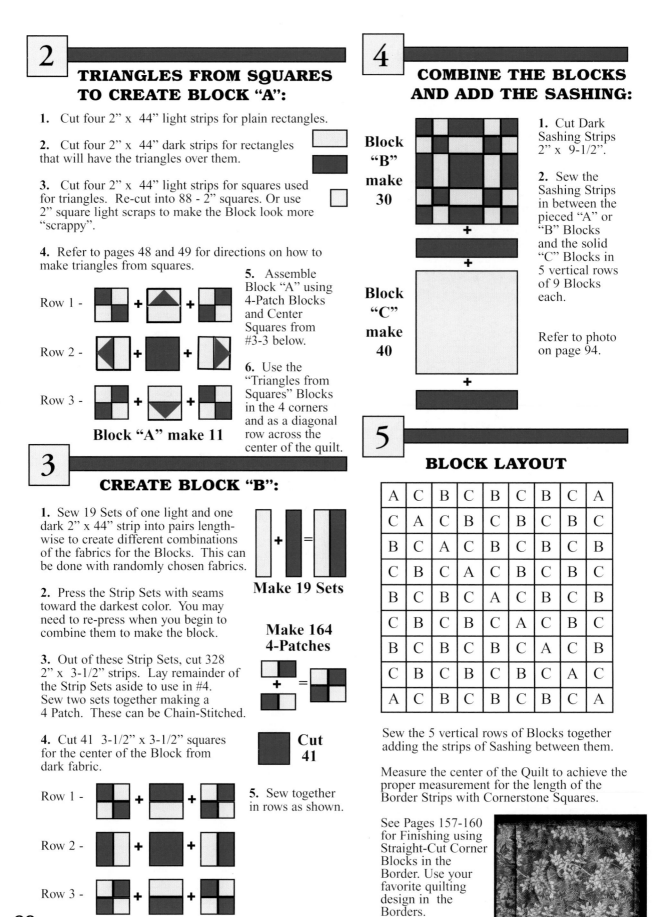

2 | TRIANGLES FROM SQUARES TO CREATE BLOCK "A":

1. Cut four 2" x 44" light strips for plain rectangles.

2. Cut four 2" x 44" dark strips for rectangles that will have the triangles over them.

3. Cut four 2" x 44" light strips for squares used for triangles. Re-cut into 88 - 2" squares. Or use 2" square light scraps to make the Block look more "scrappy".

4. Refer to pages 48 and 49 for directions on how to make triangles from squares.

Row 1 -   +   +

Row 2 -   +   +

Row 3 -   +   +

Block "A" make 11

5. Assemble Block "A" using 4-Patch Blocks and Center Squares from #3-3 below.

6. Use the "Triangles from Squares" Blocks in the 4 corners and as a diagonal row across the center of the quilt.

3 | CREATE BLOCK "B":

1. Sew 19 Sets of one light and one dark 2" x 44" strip into pairs length-wise to create different combinations of the fabrics for the Blocks. This can be done with randomly chosen fabrics.

+   =

Make 19 Sets

2. Press the Strip Sets with seams toward the darkest color. You may need to re-press when you begin to combine them to make the block.

3. Out of these Strip Sets, cut 328 2" x 3-1/2" strips. Lay remainder of the Strip Sets aside to use in #4. Sew two sets together making a 4 Patch. These can be Chain-Stitched.

Make 164 4-Patches

+   =

4. Cut 41 3-1/2" x 3-1/2" squares for the center of the Block from dark fabric.

Cut 41

Row 1 -   +   +

Row 2 -   +   +

Row 3 -   +   +

5. Sew together in rows as shown.

4 | COMBINE THE BLOCKS AND ADD THE SASHING:

Block "B" make 30

+

+

Block "C" make 40

+

1. Cut Dark Sashing Strips 2" x 9-1/2".

2. Sew the Sashing Strips in between the pieced "A" or "B" Blocks and the solid "C" Blocks in 5 vertical rows of 9 Blocks each.

Refer to photo on page 94.

5 | BLOCK LAYOUT

A	C	B	C	B	C	B	C	A
C	A	C	B	C	B	C	B	C
B	C	A	C	B	C	B	C	B
C	B	C	A	C	B	C	B	C
B	C	B	C	A	C	B	C	B
C	B	C	B	C	A	C	B	C
B	C	B	C	B	C	A	C	B
C	B	C	B	C	B	C	A	C
A	C	B	C	B	C	B	C	A

Sew the 5 vertical rows of Blocks together adding the strips of Sashing between them.

Measure the center of the Quilt to achieve the proper measurement for the length of the Border Strips with Cornerstone Squares.

See Pages 157-160 for Finishing using Straight-Cut Corner Blocks in the Border. Use your favorite quilting design in the Borders.

To create a watercolor quilt or garment fast and easy, use Deanna's Strip-Piece Method rather than the conventional techniques of cutting and piecing hundreds of two inch squares together.

It's easier to cut and sew strips than individual squares. Achieve the look of watercolor without the work of watercolor. Use the general instructions on the following pages to create two watercolor projects - one to wear and one to hang on the wall.

Stipple Quilting using Sulky Sliver Metallic #8040.

97

Deanna Spingola
Instructor, Author, Designer
Woodridge, Illinois

Deanna lives in Woodridge, Illinois with her husband. They are the proud grandparents of a growing number of grandchildren. She is the author of two books on strip-pieced watercolor and she has created a line of bargello and other quilt patterns.

Her work has been featured in numerous quilt magazines including Sew Many Quilts, Traditional Quilter and Quilting Quarterly. She teaches and lectures nationally. At home, when she is not designing and quilting, she is webmaster for a site where you can learn more about her methods:
http://www.spingola.com/ds

Strip-Pieced Watercolor Quilt & Vest

Designed & Quilted
by Deanna Spingola

Using techniques from one of her books ---
"STRIP-PIECED WATERCOLOR MAGIC"

Illustrations from the book
are used with permission of
THAT PATCHWORK PLACE
Bothell, WA.

1

SUPPLIES:
• Rotary Cutter & Mat
• 6" X 24" Quilter's Ruler
• Sewing Thread - cotton
• Seam Ripper • Pins • Safety Pins
• Post-it© Notes (size 1-1/4" x 2")
• Small Scissors or Thread Clips
• Sewing Machine
• Size 75 Machine Needle for piecing
• 1/4" Foot

2

GENERAL INSTRUCTIONS FOR STRIP-PIECED WATERCOLOR PROJECTS:

Watercolor concepts focus mostly on fabric value rather than color. You will automatically select your favorite colors when purchasing fabric for watercolor. Value is the lightness or darkness of the fabric surface.

There are three Categories of Value: light, medium and dark.

Within each of those categories there is a light and a dark: light light, dark light, light medium, dark medium, light dark and dark dark. Of course there are many variables but, for simplicity, we will use six values.

Use the accompanying Value Key, combined with the Fabric Run example, along with the fabric selection recommendations to select your fabrics for both of the strip-pieced watercolor projects.

Evaluating Value

My favorite method of initially perceiving the value of fabric is to photocopy it. Lay two of each of the six values, as you perceive them, on a copy machine. A copy machine is very objective and shows you what is light, medium and dark. It also defines the motif style. You do not need to copy every fabric you intend to use.

Fabric Value Key	
■	**Dark Dark**
▨	**Light Dark**
▦	**Dark Medium**
▨	**Light Medium**
░	**Dark Light**
□	**Light Light**

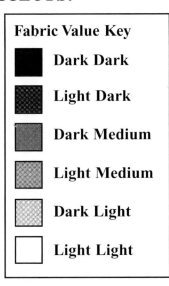

Now make 2" cuts as illustrated. Be sure to level the ruler - either with fabric or previous cuts. As you make your cuts, insert a safety pin through the back (wrong side) of the top square of each cut through all fabric layers as in the illustration. Clean cut as necessary to maintain 90° cuts. Project choice determines the number of cuts.

Close the pin. Each pin contains all the rows of the Block in their exact sewing order for your particular Project. When you are ready to sew the Block, flip the fabric cuts to the right side and open the pin. Leave the pin in and use it as a spindle. The first strip off the pin is the first row of the Block. The second strip off the pin is the second row of the Block. Seam allowances of adjacent rows will nest because of previous pressing. As you begin sewing each Block, place a small safety pin in the top left square of the first row. This is the top left of the finished Block. This pin reminds you to sew each additional row to the right side of Row #1. This pin also corresponds to the asterisks in the *Quilt Assembly Diagram.* A finished Block Assembly for the Vest should look something like the illustration.

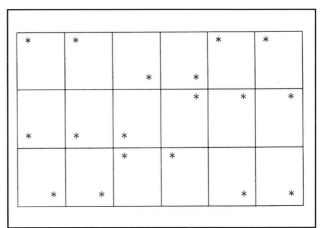

Block Assembly Diagram

In addition to General Supplies you will need:

- Vest Pattern without darts either in front or back. The length of the front and back of the Vest pattern for your size should measure 25" or under. Alter if necessary. Deanna prefers a pattern without sharp points to avoid mitering the final binding. However, these are easily altered.

- Sulky Sliver Metallic #8040
- Size 90 Topstitch Needle
- Sulky Invisible Thread
- 1 pkg. Batting
- Backing: 1-1/2 Yards
- Binding: 1/2 yard - it can be the same fabric as your backing.
- 2.5 Bias Tape Maker
- Darning Foot
- Walking Foot

- Material: 2" x 44" - Fabric Strips in the following Values:
      Light Light: 6
      Dark Light: 6
      Light Medium: 6
      Dark Medium: 6
      Light Dark: 6
      Dark Dark: 6

      Total Number: 36 Different Fabrics

The Project:
A Watercolor Fantasy Vest

CATEGORIZE YOUR FABRIC:

U 1	D 2	U 3	D 4	U 5	D 6

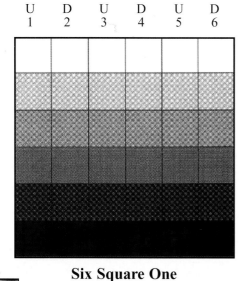

Six Square One

Categorize your fabric as in Step 1 on page 98, and lay out the Block. Evaluate and then create the six Strip Sets. Make eighteen *Cross Cuts* to create eighteen Blocks that should resemble the photo.

Use the Quilt Illustration and Block Assembly Diagram to assemble the Blocks. Rotate the Blocks as necessary. Remember the safety pins in the left top corner of each Block correspond to the asterisks in the Quilt Assembly Diagram. Assemble all the Blocks on a table or floor and determine the pressing direction of the vertical seams. If possible, press the seams in opposing directions.

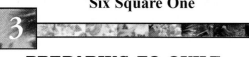

Block Assembly Diagram For Vest Fabric
*Denotes placement of safety pin in the
first square of block's strip set.

PREPARING TO QUILT:

Press the Vest Lining. Sandwich the pieced Blocks, the Batting and the Vest Lining using safety pins or your preferred method. Use muslin instead of batting for a lighter weight.

Stabilize this sandwich prior to cutting out the Vest pattern by using a walking foot and stitching in the ditch with Sulky Invisible Thread to section and stabilize the quilt into smaller, more workable areas. Now you are ready to free-motion Stipple Quilt.

Machine Set-up:
- Drop feed dogs.
- Attach a Darning Foot.
- Select straight stitch.
- Use a Topstitch Needle - Size 90.
- Put Sulky Invisible in the Bobbin.
- Thread the top with Sulky Sliver Metallic #8040 on a Vertical Spool Pin.
- Loosen Top Tension.
- Test on a scrap quilt sandwich.

Deanna loves the way that the Opalescent Sliver #8040 picks up all the various fabric colors as she stitches across them. You may want to practice on sandwiched muslin to develop your personal stippling pattern. The heavier the quilting the better it looks.

CUTTING THE PATTERN:

You will not use the outside seam allowances because all the edges of this Vest are bound. Fold back or cut off the seam allowances around all the edges and armholes on the pattern.
Warning: Do not cut off the side and shoulder seams.

Lay the front pattern piece right side up on the left edge of the pieced, quilted fabric.

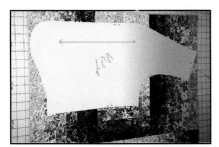

To match the side seams, mark the pattern piece where one or two seam lines fall. When you cut the second

front, align those marks to the appropriate seam lines.

After cutting out one front, flip the pattern to the wrong side and cut another one so you make both a right and left front.

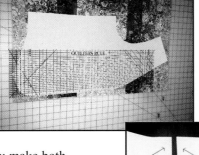

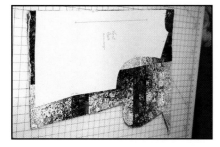

After cutting out the fronts, carefully fold the remaining quilted fabric in half as shown. Match seam allowances. Place the center back pattern piece on the fold and cut out the back. Do this even if your pattern instructs you to cut out a separate right and left back.

Lining Side Up

Sew the back and fronts together at the shoulder seams using the seam allowance called for in your pattern. Sew the side seams together.

Very lightly press all seam allowances flat.

Cut 2" bias strips for the binding. Stitch them together with a diagonal seam. The easiest way to make bias tape is to use a commercial bias tape maker and follow their package directions.

Measure and make enough binding to cover the shoulder and side seams and to go around the entire outside and armhole edges.

Hand stitch this bias binding over the inside seams. Deanna used a different lining fabric and binding fabric and created sufficient bias strips for each. Now bind the outside edges beginning on the back bottom. At the beginning of the tape, press under about 1/2". Use a 1/4" seam allowance to stitch the right side of one edge of the binding to the right side of the vest. Miter any corners as needed. Turn the binding to the inside and machine stitch *"in the ditch"* from the right side, or hand sew. Complete the armholes the same way.

103

The Project: *A Watercolor Fantasy Wall Quilt*

SUPPLIES:
- Sulky Sliver #8040
- Sulky Invisible for bobbin
- Size 90 Topstitch Needle
- Backing: 1-1/4 yards
- Borders:
  - Inside Border: 1/4 yd.
    - Cut four 1" strips from selvage to selvage.
  - Outside Border: 1/2 yd.
    - Cut four 3-1/4" strips from selvage to selvage.
- Binding: 1/3 yd.
- Batting: 41" x 41"

MATERIALS:

Strip Size: 2" x 11"

Strips
Dark Dark:	3
Light Dark:	32
Dark Medium:	11
Light Medium:	15
Dark Light:	9
Light Light:	30
Total Number	100 Different Fabrics

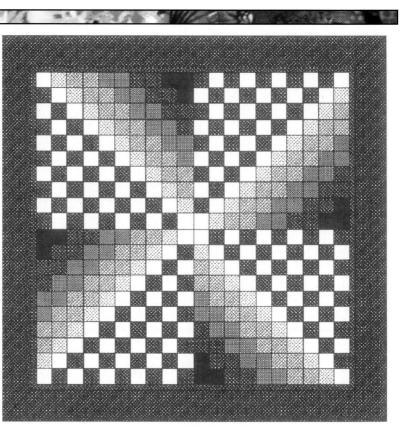

Quilt Illustration

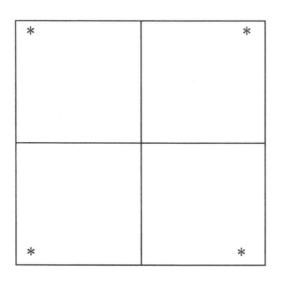

Follow the General Directions on pages 98-101 to select and lay out the fabric for the Blocks needed for the Wall Quilt.

Use the following diagram to lay out the fabrics.

CONSTRUCT & LAYOUT THE STRIP SET:

Press according to the Block Pattern, stack, *Clean Cut,* and then cut them into 2" segments.

You will probably get five cuts.

Construct the four Blocks and assemble them according to the Quilt Illustration and Block Assembly Diagram for this Block on pages 98-101. Add the borders as described on pages 157-160.

Denotes placement of safety pin in the first square of the Block's Strip Set.

U	D	U	D	U	D	U	D	U	D
1	2	3	4	5	6	7	8	9	10

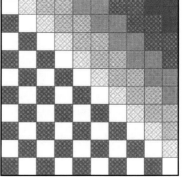

PREPARING TO QUILT:

Sandwich the finished quilt top, the batting, and the quilt backing. Pin baste with safety pins or your preferred basting method. Use a walking foot and Sulky Invisible Thread to *"stitch in the ditch"* to quarter the Quilt into smaller, more workable areas. ***Stipple Quilt*** the entire quilt with Sulky Sliver Metallic #8040. Use Sulky Invisible in the bobbin or match the backing fabric. See more details on finishing on pages 157-160.

Quilt shown below is another color version of Deanna's Quilt featuring shades of blue. It was designed by Joyce Drexler and pieced and quilted by Evelyn Howard.

Embroidered Crayon Sandpaper Art, Tiger Tee, and Wallhanging

See more examples
of Embroidered and
Quilted Crayon Art
on the next pages.

▲

Embroidered
T-Shirt and a small
Tiger Wallhanging
designed by
Carol Ingram

◄

Joyce Drexler
and
Sue Hausmann
on the
PBS TV
Sewing
Show,
AMERICA SEWS
WITH SUE
HAUSMANN.

Joyce is presenting
Embroidered
Crayon Art Tees
and Wallhanging
by Carol Ingram.

Photo by Frank Riemer

106

Carol Ingram
Artist, Designer, Sulky Instructor and
Co-author of "Dimensional
Concepts in Sulky" Book 900B-12

Carol is an accomplished artist in the Fine Arts field, including oil painting, pastels and pencil drawing. She has studied art intensively in college and under private instruction from notable national art instructors. She has taught drawing and color to elementary school age children and given private lessons. She has won many awards for her artistic works. Her background brought Carol to a cooperative designing relationship with Cactus Punch, and they have produced four top-selling computerized machine embroidery "Signature Series" cards from Carol's original artwork.

She has sewn professionally for weddings, special occasions and "Miss Teen" beauty pageants, as well as dance and clogging teams of 30 or more. Her 40 years of sewing experience has provided her with special insight into combining her love of art and textiles into a workable product.

She presently is a designer and educator for Sulky of America, has taught at Husqvarna/Viking Sewing Conventions, and does free-lance teaching at local sewing machine dealers around Florida. She was a first place winner of the Sulky Challenge in 1996. She has also contributed many exclusive designs for other Sulky books and presentations for PBS TV sewing programs such as Kaye's Quilting Friends and Sew Creative, and has showcased her designs as a guest on America Sews with Sue Hausmann.

Sandpaper Crayon Art

Every mother or grandmother has at one time or another experienced the dilemma of trying to remove a crayon stain from their child's clothing that occurred after washing and drying them with a few crayons left in pockets. We have controlled that "dreaded stain" and made a very attractive and creative design for clothing, quilts and other fabric projects with "Crayon Art".

Also, by including our children and grandchildren in some of the projects, we get to share quality time doing fun things with them.

1

SUPPLIES:

- Light-colored 65/35% polyester/cotton T-shirts (the tan color is about as dark as you can go for use with the crayons). You can transfer color on fabrics dark-to-light, but not light-to-dark.
- Sulky Totally Stable Stabilizer
- Sulky Soft 'n Sheer Stabilizer
- Sulky KK 2000 Temporary Spray Adhesive
- Ruler and Chalk Marker (Do not use air-erasable pens) since the heat from the iron will make your markings permanent.
- Embroidery Designs from Cards. (Example: Viking Tiger Card from their library)
- Sulky Thread - Rayon and Metallic (Sample used Sulky Ultra Twist Rayon for the embroideries and Metallic #7004 for border stitching)
- Crayon sharpener.
- Inexpensive, New Paint Brush - 1" to 2" wide
- Coarse-Grain Sandpaper - available in hardware stores
- Old Scissors for cutting sandpaper to size
- One large, disposable Muslin Pressing Cloth or many small cloths from scraps of muslin.
- Large Teflon Pressing Sheet
- Regular Wax Crayons or Crayola fabric crayons, not washable crayons. Fabric crayons are dull looking when you draw with them but become very bright after ironing. Regular crayons are waxy and hold the color, but when the wax is washed out, a somewhat faded stain remains. Use both kinds of crayons to get a faint, soft effect in some places and stronger color in other places (Example: Tulip Quilt on page 115).

2

APPLY TOTALLY STABLE:

To keep the T-shirt fabric flat and firm enough to draw on with crayons, iron Totally Stable on the inside over the entire front and down as far as you want the design to go. Press well. Turn it inside out and press out any wrinkles from the front.

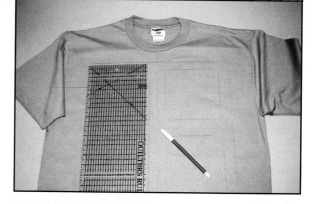

3

MARK YOUR SHIRT:

1. To center the design on the shirt, find the center front and use a chalk marker and ruler to draw a vertical line from the neck to the bottom. Measure down 1" from the neck and draw a 15" x 15" chalk square with the vertical line exactly in the center. Measure 1" inside all around the 15" square and draw four chalk 5-1/2" squares, leaving 2" between the squares.

2. Using crayons and a ruler, draw over the lines of the 15" x 15" square and all four 5-1/2" squares.

3. Using crayon, draw whatever design you wish within the 2" space between the squares.

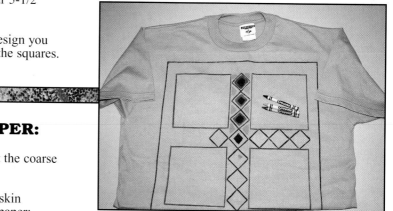

4

COLOR THE SANDPAPER:

1. With an old pair of scissors, cut the coarse sandpaper into two 5-1/2" squares.

2. Using crayons, draw an animal skin design on both squares of the sandpaper; put a lot of pressure on the crayon to push the color into the grain of the sandpaper. Cover both squares of sandpaper, edge-to-edge, with the crayon.

3. Vigorously shake the sandpaper away from the project so excess particles that have built up during the coloring process will not fall on the project.

4. Spread out the T-shirt on an ironing surface. Place the sandpaper (colored side down) inside one of the 5-1/2" squares. Use the clean paint brush to brush away any small particles of crayon that may have dropped onto the T-shirt.

SET COLOR WITH IRON:

5

Use either a large teflon pressing sheet or a new, clean, disposable muslin press cloth to cover beyond the entire surface. With an iron set on cotton, press (do not move iron) for approximately 10 seconds. Lift iron, move it, and press for 10 seconds; continue doing this until the entire 5-1/2" square has been pressed. Gently remove the press cloth and sandpaper.

REPEAT PROCESSES TO CREATE ANOTHER SQUARE:

6

Place the second square of colored sandpaper on the T-shirt, diagonally opposite from the first square. Brush away any particles of crayon with a clean brush. Cover with a new, clean press cloth, and press with an iron the same way as the first square. Remove press cloth and sandpaper.

Using a new clean muslin press cloth, large enough to cover the entire design, press the entire design once more to soak up any excess color.

EMBROIDER THE TWO OPPOSITE SQUARES:

7

Turn shirt inside out. Spray KK 2000 onto a large piece of Sulky Soft 'n Sheer and adhere it to the Totally Stable. Turn shirt right side out.

Using decorative stitches from your machine and your choice of Sulky threads, stitch around the outside of your design squares.

Use appropriate Sulky 40 wt. or Sulky 35 wt. Ultra Twist to embroider tigers or other designs in the 5-1/2" blank squares. Trim away stabilizers on back of shirt.

109

Sandpaper Seashells by the Seashore

Designs found on the pull-out pattern sheet

Designed, Colored and Quilted by Carol Ingram

1. Cut a whole cloth (60/40 poly/cotton) the size you want for your quilt top and iron Totally Stable onto the back of it.

2. Follow basic Crayon Art directions using supplies listed on page 107.

3. Enlarge to desired size and trace the SEASHELL DESIGNS (from the pull-out pattern sheet) onto Tear-Easy and cut them out for templates

4. Lightly spray KK 2000 on the Tear-Easy templates, place each one on the back of a sandpaper piece that is rough-cut slightly larger than each template, and trace the seashells onto the sandpaper.

5. Use pressure to grind the crayon into the grid of the sandpaper. Color several or all of the seashell designs.

6. Press them onto your quilt top using a hot iron and a new, clean muslin pressing cloth. Reapply the crayon to the sandpaper as needed to space the shell designs evenly all over the fabric.

7. Use an old cheese grater and crayon to speckle the entire piece of fabric, avoiding the seashell designs. (Carol used the same blue she used for the seashells, adding just a couple of sprinkles of pink.) Use a clean brush to spread particles of crayon evenly. Press entire piece with a hot iron and a Teflon pressing sheet to melt crayon specks.

8. Machine wash with mild detergent. Line dry. Press.

9. Make your quilt sandwich using KK 2000, batting and backing fabric as directed on page 69.

10. Use Sulky Rayon or Metallic Thread to free-motion stipple quilt around each seashell pattern and over entire rest of quilt. Carol used Sulky Metallic #7044 Rainbow Prism Blue.

11. Carol cut her quilt edges into a wavy pattern and bound the edges with a bias-cut binding. (Follow the instructions on page 160, but cut binding on bias for wavy edges.)

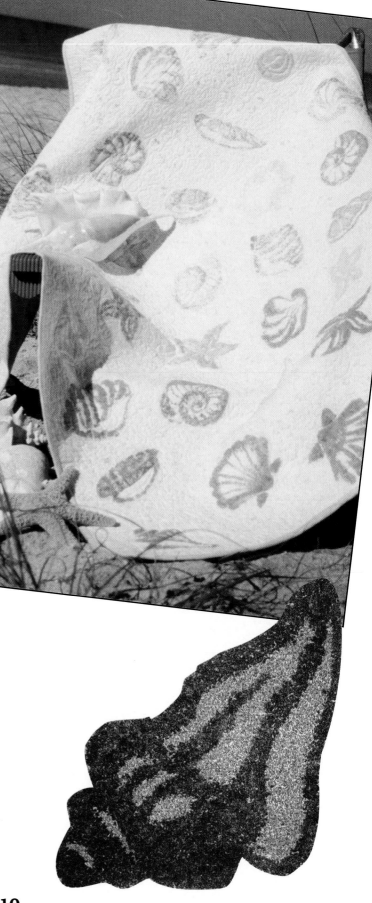

Sulky Black Stabilizer Art

Designed by Carol Ingram and Presented by Joyce Drexler on the PBS TV Show
AMERICA SEWS WITH SUE HAUSMANN

This is a great Easter project for Mom and the Kids or Grandma and Grandkids to do together; and a lot less messy than coloring eggs! Of course, you can use this technique with other images as well.

1. Cut egg-shape templates (design on pull-out pattern sheet) from **Sulky Black Totally Stable** by fan-folding the stabilizer as if you were cutting out a string of paper dolls.

2. Cut them apart and iron them onto the inside of a child's light-colored T-shirt. Have them looking happy by turning them in different directions. (See finished shirt above.)

3. Iron a large piece of **White Totally Stable** over the entire inside front of the T-shirt, covering the Black Totally Stable pieces.

4. Turn the shirt right side out with the Black Totally Stable egg shapes showing through.

5. Outline the eggs with various crayon colors and then color the rest of the egg as desired.

6. Cover the eggs with a new, clean, muslin pressing cloth and press with a hot iron for 10 seconds. Do not slide the iron; lift iron, move it, and press for 10 seconds until all of the eggs have been pressed.

7. Use Sulky 40 wt. Rayon Thread to embroider "HAPPY EASTER" lettering, either free-motion or with a computerized embroidery machine, onto the front of the shirt. For added dimension, embroider it over Sulky Puffy Foam, then tear away the excess Puffy Foam. If any "pokies" remain on the outside of the lettering, simply place a steam iron above the lettering (not directly on it) and shoot with steam to shrink the "pokies" inside the thread. Remove Totally Stable.

Noah's Embroidered Crayon Art Wallhanging

(Carol Ingram's Noah's Ark design can be found on the pull-out pattern sheet.)

Carol had her granddaughter, Tess, color in the Noah's Ark design with crayons utilizing some of the same techniques used in Garden Spot on the following page.

Evelyn drew this fabulous watering can design and colored it using Carol's crayon techniques. *(Design found on the pull-out pattern sheet.)*

She featured it on an Irish Chain Quilt which she made from a polyester blend fabric and quilted with Sulky Poly Deco Thread.

Evelyn Howard
Designer, Sample Maker for Sulky of America, and Manager of the Traveling "Sulky Challenge" Trunk Shows.

Quilted Snippet Crayon Art
The Garden Spot
Designed, Colored and Quilted by Carol Ingram

A whole-cloth, quilted wallhanging using crayons to stain the fabric, thereby creating a beautiful quilted textile painting. The crayon lays a suitable background for additional techniques such as, free-motion embroidery, Cindy Walter's "Snippet" technique or regular applique. Crayon is less messy than dyes or paints, and it lets those who wish, add an artistic touch to their textile wallhangings. Plus, it's fun.

1

SUPPLIES:

- Off-white poly/cotton fabric at least 60/40%, in whatever size you choose.
- Printed fabrics for borders and back of quilt
- Regular crayons
- Fabric crayons by Dritz (only come in 8 colors)
- Sulky Totally Stable Stabilizer
- Small pieces of fabrics about 8" x 8" in greens, pinks and blue-purples, each in at least three values from light to dark.
- Steam-A-Seam 2
- Sulky Soft 'n Sheer Stabilizer
- Permanent-ink, black marker
- Various Sulky threads for free-motion butterflies (Carol used Sulky Ultra Twist)
- Sulky Bobbin Thread
- Sulky Rayon Threads to stipple quilt
- Cotton batting 33" x 43"
- Old cheese grater and clean 1" paint brush
- Pressing mat
- Teflon Pressing Sheet
- 10" Wooden Machine Embroidery Hoop
- 12" x 12" piece of Crystal Organza
- Sulky KK 2000 Temporary Spray Adhesive
- Zig-Zag Sewing Machine
- Even Feed Foot
- Darning Foot
- Several Scrap Muslin pieces for press cloths - disposable

FINISHED MEASUREMENTS:

- Landscape format finished piece - 32" x 42"
- Image - 20" x 30"
- Borders - 1", 1-1/2", 3-1/2"
- Binding - Cut 2-1/2" strips (folded in half) for a 1/2" finished edge.
  (All should have a 1/4" seam allowance added.)

Carol prepares a small colored sketch of the design. You may get your inspiration from photographs, magazine pictures or cards. This helps you organize fabrics and colors, and is also useful to determine background, middle ground and foreground, as well as a focal point in the picture. Once the piece starts unfolding, some changes may be made, but generally Carol stays with her original sketched idea.

2

PREPARE THE FABRICS:

1. To remove any finish, wash and dry the poly/cotton fabric. (100% cotton will not hold the crayon and will fade with washing.)

2. Iron Totally Stable over the back of the entire piece of fabric to be used for the whole cloth image. It should be one piece, not several small ones, because as you draw with the crayons over the sections, you will create demarcation lines which may spoil your design.

   The Totally Stable serves two purposes. One, to act as a stabilizer and hold the fabric taut for the scrubbing when coloring with the crayons; and the other to act as a resist so the crayon will not bleed through to anything underneath during the ironing process. The Totally Stable should be ironed on very well from both sides and all wrinkles ironed out.

3. Prepare "Snippet" fabrics by cutting them into 8" x 8" pieces and applying Steam-A-Seam 2 to the back. Set aside to use later.

113

3

USING THE CRAYONS:

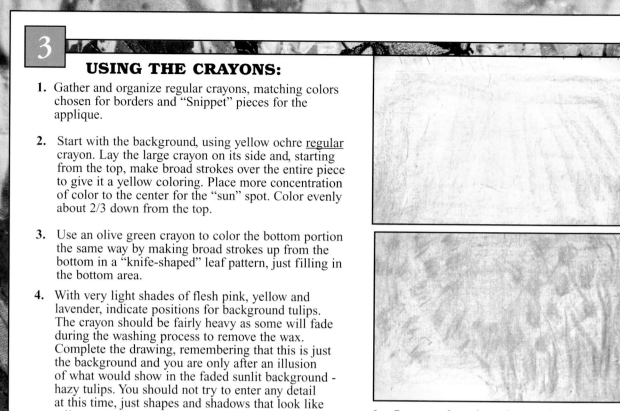

1. Gather and organize regular crayons, matching colors chosen for borders and "Snippet" pieces for the applique.

2. Start with the background, using yellow ochre <u>regular</u> crayon. Lay the large crayon on its side and, starting from the top, make broad strokes over the entire piece to give it a yellow coloring. Place more concentration of color to the center for the "sun" spot. Color evenly about 2/3 down from the top.

3. Use an olive green crayon to color the bottom portion the same way by making broad strokes up from the bottom in a "knife-shaped" leaf pattern, just filling in the bottom area.

4. With very light shades of flesh pink, yellow and lavender, indicate positions for background tulips. The crayon should be fairly heavy as some will fade during the washing process to remove the wax. Complete the drawing, remembering that this is just the background and you are only after an illusion of what would show in the faded sunlit background - hazy tulips. You should not try to enter any detail at this time, just shapes and shadows that look like tulips.

5. When finished, lay a piece of scrap muslin over the top and PRESS each area for at least 10 to 15 seconds to melt the crayon wax into the fabric. Do not slide the iron, press and lift the iron. DO NOT USE THIS CLOTH AGAIN since the crayon will transfer to another piece, giving you tulips where you don't want them.

6. Once you have ironed your piece, re-evaluate the coloring and make any adjustments to the design with your crayons, and then re-press. When you are happy with the design, remove the Totally Stable and wash with mild detergent, no bleach, and warm water to remove the wax residue left by the crayons. Line dry. Press. Reapply Totally Stable to the entire back.

4

CREATE THE DESIGN USING SNIPPETS OF FABRIC:

Carol suggests that you use a large June Tailor Pressing Mat so you don't have to disturb your design while working with the small "Snippet" pieces.

1. Start with the light values of the green leaf color and make large cuttings, creating long, knife-shaped leaves. Begin at the middle ground and place the leaves with the fusible side down; choose the middle value of green and then the darkest value in the immediate foreground. This creates depth with the darkest value in the foreground which gradually recedes to the background toward the greatest light. Make large angular cuttings of the darkest values of the blue-purples and pinks to make the tulips in the foreground.

2. The shapes should be largest in the foreground and gradually get smaller as you place them in the background toward the light. The theory being, large shapes and dark bold colors belong in the foreground that gradually get smaller and paler in the background, disappearing into the light.

3. Once the cut pieces are as you like them, cover them with a Teflon pressing sheet and press everything down.

114

5

EVALUATE YOUR PAINTING:

1. If any crayon leaves or stems are needed, add them now. Also, you may want to add a slight amount of detail on some of the crayon tulips for effect. During this process you may want to use the "Fabric" crayons, since they are <u>much bolder in color when ironed</u>.

2. If the background is too faint, adding touches of the bolder color ties the foreground and background together. Carol prefers a combination of both regular and fabric crayons. If you added any crayon, press again with a new, clean muslin pressing cloth.

6

ADD THE SPECKLED EFFECT:

To create the speckled effect, use an old cheese grater and two colors of crayon (Carol used two shades of purple). Grate small particles of both colors over the entire image, except the sunlit portion. Use the clean paint brush to scatter the particles evenly so concentration is mainly on the leaf and flower sections. Cover with a Teflon pressing sheet and melt the specks onto the image with a hot iron. Do not use a fabric pressing cloth since the cloth will just absorb the particles of crayon. The Teflon resists the crayon and forces it to melt onto your image.

115

EMBROIDERING:

1. Leave the Totally Stable in place on the back of the image and add the sashing pieces. Since the Totally Stable helps to square up the painting during the rotary cutting and prevents the seams from being distorted while handling the fabric, leave it in place until all embroidery and applique work is completed.

2. Use a permanent-ink, black marker to trace the butterflies from the pattern (found on the pull out pattern sheet) onto Soft 'n Sheer Stabilizer. Place it in a wooden machine embroidery hoop and free-motion embroider the butterflies with Sulky 35 wt. Ultra Twist Rayon. Carol used #3003, #3005, #3006, #3009, #3011, #3021 and #3049. When complete, cut the butterflies away from the Soft 'n Sheer, leaving a 1/8" allowance all around the edges of the butterflies. Spray the back with KK 2000 and, using the photo as a guide for placement, applique the butterflies with Sulky 40 wt. Rayon #1005 Black onto the crayon design using a narrow satin stitch. Leave a small opening to stuff a slight amount of fiberfill inside to make the butterflies more dimensional; then stitch opening closed with a small zig-zag stitch.

3. Use a 12" x 12" piece of Crystal Organza in the same manner to free-motion embroider the dragonfly. Using the organza allows the wings to become translucent. Place the dragonfly slightly outside the design, overlapping onto the border for effect. Applique the dragonfly with

Sulky Sliver #8051 Black onto the crayon design using a narrow satin stitch.

8

QUILTING:

1. Lay the backing wrong side up and spray it with Sulky KK 2000. Place the cotton batting on top of the backing. Spray the wrong side of the quilt top with KK 2000 and place it right side up on top of the batting. Now you have a quilting sandwich.

2. Stipple quilt over the entire image with Variegated Sulky 30 wt. Rayon or 35 wt. Ultra Twist Threads. Carol used a green Sulky Ultra Twist #3017 for the leaf area and a lighter yellow Ultra Twist #3012 for the light area. Sulky Sliver #8016 was used to add sparkle to the tulips.

3. Use an even-feed foot to stitch-in-the-ditch along the seam between the image and the border with Sulky Polyester Clear Invisible Thread.

4. Bind edges and make a hanging sleeve. Apply label. Hang your quilt and enjoy!

Crayon Art Winter Snow Scene
(19" x 32" without borders)
Designed by Carol Ingram

A whole-cloth, quilted wallhanging that depicts a winter forest snow scene scattered with large and small embroidered, whimsical snowmen. The background was achieved by scrubbing-in and ironing crayon over a light-colored poly/cotton fabric. With the addition of "Snippet" pieces of fabric for texture on the trees and snow, the forest scene comes alive with depth and composition. By also adding the textures of quilting, the snowmen literally come alive as a "Snow Family" of happy characters in their natural environment.

1

SUPPLIES:

- Poly/cotton whole-cloth (one piece) fabric the size you want for your quilt
- Backing fabric larger than quilt top to accommodate borders and batting
- 1-1/2" dark blue strips for inner border, length determined by your quilt
- 2-1/2" dark blue strips for binding
- 3-1/2" medium blue strips for outer border
- Low-Loft Batting
- Regular Crayons
- Fabric Crayons
- 2 yds. Sulky Totally Stable Iron-On Stabilizer
- 2 yds. Sulky Tear-Easy Stabilizer
- Sulky KK 2000 Temporary Spray Adhesive
- 8" x 8" squares or scraps of fabric in whites, light blues, browns and ochres.

- Several scrap muslin pieces for press cloths - disposable
- Lightweight Fusible Web
- Cactus Punch Embroidery Card "Snow Family"#22 and "Winter Scenes" #23- *designed by Carol Ingram*
- Sulky 40 wt. Rayon Threads in colors indicated in embroidery cards
- Sulky Puffy Foam in colors indicated in embroidery cards
- Sulky Original Metallic Thread #7021 Prism White

See the pull-out pattern sheet for the pattern, plus the inspiration behind the design of each snowperson.

Instructions follow on next page.

INSTRUCTIONS:
SEE PULL-OUT PATTERN SHEET
Enlarge the design by 143% to 19" x 32".

1. Iron Sulky Totally Stable over the entire back of the poly/cotton fabric.

2. Using shades of blue, light to dark, lay crayon on its side and, with broad strokes, cover the sky area, working boldly at the top and lighter as you get to the middle horizon line. Using various shades of blue, light to middle values, indicate snow hills, following the pattern sheet as a guide.

3. Using both fabric crayons and regular crayons in shades of brown, ochre and rust, lay in the trees in the foreground and background, and make small patches of brown grass in the snow.

4. Using shades of olive and leaf green, indicate the horizon line by scattering fir trees along that line. Place larger fir trees in the middle ground on the right-hand side. Lay green crayon on its side and scrub in the bold tree leaf-tops in the foreground above the previously drawn trees in the foreground. This area can just be filled in, leaving a few sparse areas of blue sky, as they will be covered in the steps below with "Snippets" of snow fabric.

5. When finished, lay a piece or several pieces of scrap muslin over the top and PRESS each area for at least 10 to 15 seconds to melt the crayon wax into the fabric. Do not slide the iron, press and lift the iron. DO NOT USE THIS CLOTH AGAIN since the crayon will transfer to another piece, giving you images where you don't want them.

6. Once you have ironed your piece, re-evaluate the coloring and make any adjustments to the design with your crayons, and then re-press. When you are happy with the design, remove the Totally Stable and wash with mild detergent, no bleach, and warm water to remove the wax residue left by the crayons. Line dry. Press. Reapply Totally Stable to the entire back.

7. Select fabrics for "Snippet" pieces: green for the leaves; white for the snow on the tree tops; light blues for snow on the hills; browns and ochres for the tree trunks. Apply fusible web to the back of chosen fabrics.

8. Starting with the tree trunks and placing fusible sides down, snip the browns and place them over the trunks until you have the desired tree-bark effect. Do the green leaves of the foreground trees, then the snow laid on top of the leaves. Add a few snips of white fabric(s) to the snow mounds to give them depth. Do small sections at a time and press as you go so your smaller pieces will not move around during your designing.

When the background is completed to your taste, add the borders while the Totally Stable is still in place helping to maintain the straight-of-grain. (See pages 157-160.)

ADD THE EMBROIDERIES:

1. Stabilize the area to be embroidered by using 4 layers of Sulky Tear-Easy, sprayed with KK 2000 between each layer to make a stabilizer "sandwich".

2. Embroider the Snowmen of your choice using Sulky 40 wt. Rayon Threads and Sulky Puffy Foam as indicated on the embroidery card: Dink's hat, Uncle Albert's scarf, and Betty Lou's scarf and hat. Remove Tear-Easy.

The snowmen on Carol's design are, in the foreground left to right: Uncle Albert and Jake (the cat), Granny Flowers, and Betty Lou (mirror-imaged). In the middle ground center is the Chorus Group: Lil' Louie, Dink, Dewberry and Clem; to their right is the Alaskan Fir; to their left stands Good Ol' Uncle Lester; in the middle-ground left is Lil' Louie. In the background left stands Dink, and on the horizon line are the Forest Trees.

COMPLETING YOUR QUILT:

1. Lay the backing, right side down, on a hard, flat surface. Tape or clip in place, holding fabric taut but not stretching it. Spray the wrong side of the backing fabric with KK 2000. Smooth batting over it. Spray the wrong side of the quilt top with KK-2000 and smooth over batting. Smaller wallhangings will not require any pinning. If you have oversized the scene, you may want to place a few pins to prevent any shifting while quilting.

2. To define the sky area from the snow, use Sulky Metallic #7021, Prism White to stipple-quilt the entire sky area including over the snow-covered treetops; stop at the horizon line.

3. Free-motion quilt the snow-mound areas with a side-to-side straight stitch, keeping the lines predominantly horizontal while easing down that area with a flowing, even motion. Echo quilt around the snowmen to give them more dimension.

4. Add binding (see page 160).

Pieced Embroidered Art

"Starry Night Snow Scene"

Designed, Pieced and Embroidered by
Carol Ingram who showed it on the PBS TV Show
AMERICA SEWS WITH SUE HAUSMANN

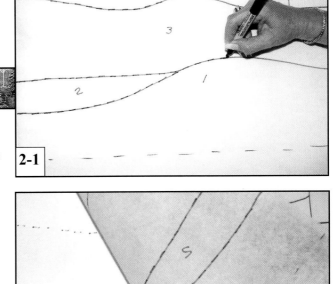

2-1

SUPPLIES & FABRICS:

- Computerized Embroidery Machine
- Cactus Punch Embroidery Card, Winter Scenes #23 *designed by Carol Ingram*
- Colors of Sulky 40 wt. Rayon and Sulky Original Metallic as recommended on Cactus Punch Card
- Sulky Polyester Invisible Clear Thread
- 20" x 24" piece of Sulky Totally Stable
- Sulky Tear-Easy Stabilizer
- One 9" x 45" piece each of 5-9 assorted Blue Snow Theme Fabrics
- 8" x 45" Medium Blue fabric for Outside Border
- 1-1/2" x 45" Navy Blue fabric for Inner Border
- 9" x 45" Green Fabric for Trees - Batiks or Mottled
- Fusible Web for Tree Appliques
- Spray Starch or Fabric Sizing
- 20" x 24" Posterboard - available at office supply stores
- Permanent-Ink, Fine-Line Marker
- Permanent-Ink, Broad Marker
- Iron & Ironing Surface • Rotary Cutter & Mat

2-1

PREPARE CARDBOARD TEMPLATES & FABRIC PIECES:

1. Spray pattern (from pull-out pattern sheet) with KK 2000 and cover it with Tear-Easy. Trace the pattern onto the Tear-Easy with a fine-line, permanent-ink marker. Spray the poster board with KK 2000 and adhere the Tear-Easy to it. Use a broad-point, permanent-ink marker to trace over the lines on the Tear-Easy with short dashes that will bleed through the Tear-Easy onto the poster board. Re-draw these lines solidly on the poster board by connecting the dots with the broad-point marker. Number the sequence of templates on the poster board. Cut out the poster board templates. Make your fabric choice for each template.

2. Lay a poster board template on each chosen fabric, numbered side down to wrong side of fabric. Trace around each template with a pencil or chalk marker, allowing a 1/4" seam allowance on the top and bottom edges of each fabric piece. Cut out.

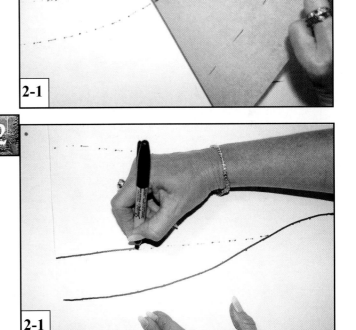

2-1

3. To stiffen the fabric and make the edges crisp and easy to sew, spray starch the back of each cut-out fabric piece and lay the matching poster board template, numbered side down, on the wrong side of the fabric. With a hot iron, press the 1/4" top and bottom edges over the poster board until dry. Repeat for all pieces.

4. On a pressing surface, lay the 20" x 24" piece of Totally Stable, fusible side up, on top of the original pattern so the design shows through.

119

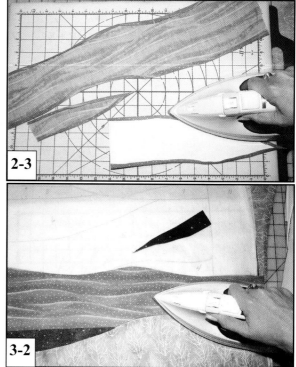

Finished Size: 24-1/4" H x 25-1/4" W

Layout design can be found on the pull-out pattern sheet.

LAY OUT THE SCENE ON SULKY TOTALLY STABLE:

1. Remove poster board from each fabric piece and re-press well. Lay each piece in numbered sequence on Totally Stable, butting the pressed-down edges together. Do not overlap.

2. Press as you go, two pieces at a time. When all pieces are assembled, press well again. **Do not** touch the iron to the exposed Totally Stable.

EMBROIDER & QUILT IT:

1. Thread machine with Sulky Polyester Clear Invisible on top and bobbin. Catching both fabrics, sew all seams very close to the butted edges with a 1.5 to 2.0 width zig-zag at a length of 1.0 to 1.5.
2. Sew on borders.
3. Stabilize the underside with four layers of Tear-Easy and use Sulky Rayons and Metallics to embellish with embroideries from the "Winter Scenes" Card.
4. Trace trees from pull-out pattern sheet onto the fusible web. Apply fusible web to wrong side of green tree fabric. Cut out and fuse where desired on the scene. Putting a tree on the border is a nice touch. Free-motion straight stitch over trees with a dark green Sulky Ultra Twist Rayon Thread that matches your tree fabric.
5. Square outside edges and construct the quilt as desired. Quilt it with Sulky Sliver #8040.

120

Denim Acrylic/Embroidered Art

Designed & Painted
by Carol Ingram

SUPPLIES:

- A ready-made jeans jumper, jacket, vest or skirt
- Artist™ Acrylic Paints: tree green, olive green, white, dark brown, yellow ochre
- Cactus Punch Cards - Snow Family #22 and Winter Scenes #23
- Sulky 40 wt. Rayon and Sulky Metallic Thread colors as recommended on Cactus Punch Cards
- Artist's stiff boar's bristle brushes
- Sulky Sticky and Tear-Easy Stabilizers
- Fabric Pens - Brown or Black
- Sulky 2 mm Puffy Foam

PREPARE THE GARMENT:

Prewash the garment to remove any excess dye and fabric sizing. Press. To stiffen the fabric and keep it flat while painting, adhere Sulky Sticky on the inside of the garment in the area where you wish to paint a scene, usually along the bottom edge of the garment.

Use a tree-green paint and large boar's bristle brush to scrub in an underpainting of irregular fir-tree shaped trees along an invisible horizon line at the lower edge of your garment. Paint some larger trees in the foreground and some smaller trees in the background, creating depth in the forest. Use white paint along the horizon line under the trees to scrub in some areas of snow mounds in the foreground.

When the under-painting of the first painted green trees is somewhat dry, use a lighter olive green to restate those tree shapes and create individual limbs. Use white to place some snow caps on the top of the limbs.

A large feature tree may be painted in the foreground starting with dark brown and adding yellow ochre highlights.

Finish your Wearable Snow Scene by using Sulky Tear-Easy Stabilizer and Sulky Rayon and Metallic Threads to machine embroider the large and small snowmen designs from Cactus Punch Cards #22 Snow Family and #23 Winter Scenes.

Using dark brown or black fabric pens, draw trees in between the trees. In the far background, draw some smaller twiggy dead trees to fill in.

These garments may be turned inside out and washed by themselves on the delicate cycle in a washing machine with mild detergent; line dry. Iron from the reverse side with steam and medium heat so as not to disturb the paint. Do not iron over the paint on the front side.

Designed & Quilted by Joyce Drexler
Presented on the PBS TV Show,
"SEW CREATIVE" with Donna Wilder

Fabric Credits: Timeless Treasures
Collection plus mottled solids
by Patrick Lose for
Hi-Fashion Fabrics

Marsh Ducks Landscape

✂ Cutting Guide:

Always cut the selvages off the fabric before cutting strips.

Cut 1/4 yard pieces of each:

- ✂ Sky - Cloudy/Stormy
- ✂ Hills - Black, Slate and Spruce
- ✂ Forest - Pattern Buck 2 Winter
- ✂ Marsh/Ducks - Pattern Misty 2 Winter
- ✂ Deer - Pattern Buck 1 Winter
- ✂ Border - Pattern 1006/Slate
- ✂ Backing and Binding - Pattern Eden 2 Winter

SUPPLIES:

- One 20" x 24" piece of Sulky Cut-Away Plus Permanent Stabilizer for the foundation

- **Sulky 30 wt. Rayon Threads:**
  1005 - Black Hills
  1162 - Slate Hills
  1046 - Spruce Hills

- **Sulky 35 wt. Rayon Ultra Twist Thread:**
  3010 - Grasses

- **Sulky Sliver Metallic:**
  8040 - Snow/Clouds and to
  Quilt Ducks and Tree Tops
  8051 - Tree Trunks
  8006 - Deer Outline and Tops of Trees

- Sulky Polyester Invisible Thread for the bobbin
- Zig-zag Sewing Machine
- Free-Motion Darning Foot
- Embroidery or Metallic Needle 14/90

NOTIONS:

- Rotary Cutter, Mat and Ruler
- Sulky KK 2000 Temporary Spray Adhesive
- 1 to 2 yards Steam-A-Seam 2 Double-Sided Fusible Web or Fine Fuse™ and Teflon Pressing Sheet
- Ironing Surface and Steam Iron
- Sharp Pointed Scissors
- 8" or 10" German Wooden Machine Embroidery Hoop (optional)
- Quilter's Pins
- Fine-Line, Permanent-Ink Marker
- 21" x 25" piece of Fairfield Low-Loft Batting or two layers of Fleece
- Optional Jacket Pattern *(page 125)* *"Fringed Cardigan Jacket"* Linda Crone Creations To order by mail call: 815-654-9601.

PREPARE THE FOUNDATION & FABRIC PIECES:

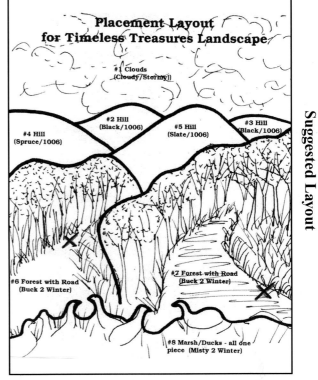

Suggested Layout

1. Use the 20" x 24" piece of Sulky Cut-Away Plus for the landscape wallhanging foundation. If making the landscape to be used as the fabric in a vest or jacket, layout the pieces on pre-shrunk muslin or flannel.

2. **Prepare the Fabric Landscape Applique Pieces:** Apply a 1" to 2" strip of fusible web (Steam-A-Seam 2) all across the top edge of the wrong side of the clouds, hills, forest and marsh fabrics. (We suggest only a small strip since a large amount of fusible can make your piece stiffer. This is extremely important when using the landscape as an inset on a garment where we suggest using Fine Fuse over the entire piece.) Rough cut the deer and apply fusible web to the back of the entire piece. Remove the release paper when trimming is complete in #5.

3. Refer to the layout above and begin positioning the fabrics of the landscape from the top of the landscape and work down. Once an area is cut as desired, spray the entire back of the cut piece with Sulky KK 2000 Temporary Spray Adhesive and place it on the foundation as desired. The KK 2000 will allow you to reposition the piece as needed. <u>Do not press</u> until entire landscape has been placed.

3

1. Using a rotary cutter, mat and ruler, cut a piece of sky fabric that will cover the top 1/4 to 1/3 of your wall-hanging. Be sure clouds are billowing UP, not down.

2. "Free-hand" rotary cut two pieces of the forest to reach all the way across the piece, making sure to have a road featured in the right-hand 1/3 of the landscape; the tree tops should be sloping as they move along the piece. The roads are ideal places to put deer. Sometimes cutting the tree sections, altering their height and layering them is also effective if you don't have yardage. Make sure trees are standing straight.

4

1. It is imperative that you have fusible web behind these half-cut duck shapes, and that none of the actual duck's heads are cut off. Cut the marsh duck fabric using sharply pointed scissors so you can easily cut around the dark blue duck heads for added interest.

The marsh and forest combined should make up 3/4 of the landscape.

2. "Free-hand" rotary cut rounded, fluid, rolling hill shapes from the three mottled fabrics suggested. (See the layout on page 123.) Joyce liked the Black as the farthest hill, the Slate, and then the Spruce. Do not cut them all the same size. Vary the size

and shape for interest. (Be sure that you still have enough fusible web left on the hills to fuse the top edge down after you cut. If not, reapply.) Our layout is only a suggestion. *As you can see in various photos, each example varies.*

5

1. Finally, detail-cut your deer. Do not cut away any of the actual deer, but rather just outside the shape. Choose deer by size and direction they are facing. Always have them facing in toward the center of the landscape. Have the larger deer in the foreground along the side of the road so you can add stitched grass under them later as shown above. If you can find appropriately sized embroidery deer designs or you have scanning and digitizing capabilities, you can add embroidered deer instead of fabric ones. ("X" on the placement layout sheet shows where Joyce added deer.) Joyce suggests you save a large deer until after the border strips have been added, then place it slightly overlapping into the border for interest.

2. Layer the pieces and fuse them down. Beginning at the top of the Landscape Scene, if you haven't already done so, remove the fusible backing paper. Reapply the KK 2000, if needed, to temporarily hold the pieces in place until you are certain that everything is overlapping.

Work your way from top to bottom, starting with the clouds. Make this a fun adventure. Don't be afraid to play with your fabric pieces. By using the double-stick fusible web and KK 2000 you can reposition the pieces over and over again before doing the final fuse.

3. Once you are satisfied with the placement of all your applique pieces, fuse them down. **Steam press well.**

EMBROIDER THE LANDSCAPE:

You can also use decorative stitches from your machine with the feed dogs feeding as Patsy Shields did on her jacket below.

1. Thread your machine with either an appropriate color of Sulky Rayon Thread or Sulky Polyester Invisible Thread, attach an edge foot, and stitch down all the cut edges with one row of straight stitching to act as a basting stitch.

2. Set up your machine for free-motion work:
   • Lower the feed dogs.
   • Attach a free-motion darning foot or quilting foot.
   • Insert a new Embroidery or Metallic Needle, size 14/90.
   • Thread the top with Sulky Sliver #8040 Opalescent. Use Sulky Clear or Smoke Invisible Polyester Thread in the bobbin (wind your bobbin slowly).
   • Select a straight stitch.
   • Loosen your top tension substantially until no bobbin thread is pulled to the top of the work. (On some machines, you may need to lower it to near "0" when using Sulky Sliver Thread.
   • Place a section of the sky fabric in a wooden machine embroidery hoop. Or, do not use a hoop if you are experienced at free-motion and prefer more access to the design.
   • Begin free-motion embellishing over the landscape fabrics.

Sky: Use a straight stitch and a side-stitch outlining motion with Sulky Sliver Opalescent #8040 to add a light, open outline around some of the cloud shapes. Keep the sky horizontal at all times and simply ease around the shapes, feathering into them with a side-stitch motion.

Marsh Water: Use a straight stitch and a free-motion side stitch to add shimmering Sliver #8040 to the water pools in the marsh.

125

Cut-Edge of Tree Tops: Add several rows of straight stitching using Sliver #8006 along the cut edge.

Deer: Use a free-motion straight stitch to outline the deer and antlers with Sliver #8006. (If you wish to have the deer overlap the border, wait to apply the large deer until the border is added.)

Hills: Continue straight stitch, side-stitching using the appropriate color of Sulky 30 wt. Rayon along the cut edges of the hills. Hills can also have distant trees by using a varied zig-zag stitch along edge.

Trunks of Trees: Thread up with Black Sliver #8051 and add some free-motion straight stitching to the darkest trunks of the trees.

Grass Tufts: Using Sulky Ultra Twist #3010, add some free-motion straight stitching to the marsh grasses.

7 FINISH THE LANDSCAPE:

1. Trim the embroidered landscape to 18" x 22".

2. Use a 1/2" seam allowance to add 2" to 4" wide border strips, depending on your desired finished size. Press. Add deer to border, if desired.

3. Place the backing fabric right side down and spray with Sulky KK 2000. Next, add a layer of Low-Loft batting or two layers of fleece. Then, spray the wrong side of the embellished landscape with KK 2000. Place the landscape right side up over the batting or fleece. Baste from corner to corner in an "X".

4. With a free-motion straight stitch, outline once around each of the shapes using the suggested color and type of thread above. Outline stitch around the darkest ducks using Sliver Opalescent #8040.

5. Cut binding 2-1/2" wide. Fold binding strips in half lengthwise, wrong sides together. Place the raw edges of the binding to the raw edge of the border and sew them together with a 1/4" seam allowance. Turn fold to back and hand-stitch it to the backing.

   Note - when making a garment from this landscape, it is important to cover the cut edges of the appliqued pieces more thoroughly than on a wallhanging. You might want to use decorative stitches from your sewing machine that are quite dense. Straight stitching is not adequate for garments that will be handled a great deal and laundered from time to time.

Tessellating Star

Designed and Quilted by Jackie Robinson

"For machine quilting, the resulting effect is enhanced when the threads are doing some extra work as well. A few years ago, I discovered Sulky's Sliver thread, finding the sparkle it adds exciting, and the thread easy to work with. Because it's a continuous fiber, not a twist, it flows through the needle without snapping, even at high speed. What a joy to quilt with!"
---Jackie

Sulky Sliver Metallic Thread was used to quilt this Tessellating Star that was designed, pieced and quilted by Jackie Robinson.

Fabrics used:
Navy - Maywood "One World 2000"
White - Maywood "Beautiful Backgrounds"

To order the "Tessellations" book, contact:
Animas Quilts Publishing
P.O. Box 693
Durango, CO 81302
970-247-4549
e-mail: AnimasQuilts
Publishing@Animas.com
http://www.animas.com

Jackie Robinson

Author, Designer, Educator
Durango, CO

Jackie Robinson lives near Durango, Colorado, where she owns Animas Quilts Publishing and formerly owned a well-known quilt shop, Animas Quilts.

Although not a native to Colorado, she "got here as fast as she could", but she finds herself happily on the road regularly, teaching and lecturing here and abroad.

Quilting since the 70's, Jackie's work has been featured in several magazines, most recently the Sampler issue of American Patchwork & Quilting, June 1997; Quilters Newsletter Magazine, December 1997; and Quiltmaker, Nov-Dec 1997; Patchwork Quilt Tsushin, April 1998; Australian Patchwork & Quilting, June 1998; and Quilting Today, October 1998. She's the author of eleven books on quiltmaking, as well as numerous patterns.

In the classroom, Jackie's students are treated to the specific techniques involved in their class, and also to precision piecing tricks as well as efficient shortcuts which help to streamline the pleasures of quiltmaking, allowing time for MORE!

Tessellating Light to Dark Star

The word Tessellate means "to form with mosaic". The edges of each "design" form the edges of its neighboring design. The pattern of designs could go on into infinity, knowing no apparent borders. The well-known Dutch artist, M.C. Escher, 1898-1972, developed the tessellating design process to new heights in his Symmetry works and Metamorphose pieces. This design, taken from Jackie's book, TESSELLATIONS is based on the same principle, but scaled to ease with machine piecing.

✂ Cutting Guide

Always cut the selvages off the fabric before cutting strips.

YARDAGE: (based on top quality 42-45" 100% cotton fabrics)

- ✂ 3-1/8 yards Dark (includes binding)
- ✂ 3-1/8 yards Light (includes binding)
- ✂ 3-5/8 yards Backing

of EACH of the dark and light fabric, cut:
- ✂ 4 Strips 5" - save for borders
- ✂ 4 Strips 2-1/2" - save for binding
- ✂ 35 Strips 2", into:
- ✂ 165 - 2" x 3-1/2"
- ✂ 165 - 2" x 5"

CONSTRUCT THE BLOCKS

Stitch with accurate, scant 1/4" seams throughout.

Place the 2" x 3-1/2" segments of Light perpendicular on top of the same size Dark, and stitch diagonally as shown. (The angle is very important -- do it exactly as shown!)

CREATE THE QUILT TOP:

1. Add the 2" x 5" pieces above and below this unit as shown.

2. Make 165 of these blocks and arrange as in the drawing, 11 blocks x 15 blocks. Stitch together.

3. See pages 157-160 for more on finishing. Add borders by stitching the light to the top and the dark to the bottom, leaving at least 5-1/2" extending for the miter. Likewise, attach the side borders, also leaving the extension for mitering.

4. Miter the upper left and lower right border corners.

5. Echo quilt (see page 10) with Sulky Sliver Metallic and bind, placing light binding along the light borders, and dark on the dark sides.

"Ethan's Baby Quilt"

Pieced and Quilted by Joyce Drexler, "Grandma" to Ethan Noe. Noah's Ark was the theme for Ethan's Baby Shower since Noah is sometimes spelled Noe in the Bible. And Joyce actually had it quilted on time!

Quilted with Sulky Ultra Twist Rayon Thread #3034 using a feather stitch. Then to give Ethan some warm fuzzies, Joyce tied the center of each block with some coordinating yarn.

*Fabric Credit:
Debbie Mumm's
M & M Noah's Ark Collection
by South Seas Imports.*

For more Tessellating Quilt Patterns, look for Jackie's Book at your nearest Quilt Shop.

A Quick Quilted Project
The Tie That Binds

Mini-Purses from Men's Ties

Designed and Constructed by Patti Lee.

Presented by Joyce Drexler on the PBS TV Sewing program, SEW CREATIVE with Donna Wilder

A great way to use special neckties that may be outdated but are too good to give away, or they have a sentimental value. Patti says "After my husband died, I kept putting off giving his ties away. Then I was inspired to make these little purses from his ties and give them to our daughters. Young women today love small purses. They don't seem to have the need to haul everything they own around with them like my generation did. It's a wonderful little dress-up purse with just enough room for lipstick, a little money and a credit card...the essentials. I hope you enjoy making these little bags as much as I did. They're fast and easy; you can make one in less than an hour."

1

SUPPLIES:

- Necktie (minimum width at widest point - 3-1/2" to 4")
- Sulky Original Metallic and Sliver Metallic Threads
- Sulky 40 wt. Rayon Threads if using a computerized embroidery design
- Sulky Polyester Invisible Thread
- Chalk marker
- Velcro dots or patches
- Rat tail cording or other decorative cords for strap (or make a self-fabric strap)
- Fasturn tool (for turning self-fabric strap) - Optional
- Silk flowers or buttons for embellishment - Optional

2

CREATE FABRIC FROM A TIE:

1. Determine cutting length: 12-1/2" for a narrow tie - up to 16-1/2" for widest tie. Measuring from tip, mark cutting line with a chalk marker. Cut.

   (Set cut-off portion of tie aside for use later if you wish to make a matching strap.)

2. For a cleaner finish, serge or zig-zag the cut end of the tie using a small width.

Patti Lee and Rex
Englewood, FL

Patti Lee has been involved with Speed Stitch and Sulky of America first as a volunteer, then working part-time, and now on a full-time basis since both companies were formed. She is currently Consumer Relations Director for Sulky of America. She was a National Instructor for Speed Stitch and an active participant in all nine of their annual S.M.A.R.T. events. She has also worked in retail sewing machine and fabric stores. In addition to being a contributor to several "Concepts in Sulky" books, she also acts as Joyce Drexler's Creative Assistant and best friend.

Rex is Patti's Assistant. It is his job to lay on everything she is working on at the moment. He does it flawlessly.

3

EMBELLISH IT:

Embellishing suggestions using beautiful Sulky Rayons and/or Metallic Threads:

- Use either free-motion stitching, straight stitching on the diagonal, or decorative stitches using the tie fabric as a guide.

- If you have a computerized embroidery machine, you could place a design in the center of the widest area of the tie. Use two layers of Sulky Sticky under the computerized machine embroidery hoop to hold the tie for embroidery. Sulky Sticky is ideal for allowing small items to be embroidered that can't be held in a hoop.

  This design is from the New Home Memory Card #16 - Cat Series.

4

CONSTRUCT IT:

1. Fold down 1/2" on the narrow, cut end of the tie. To make the channel to slip the strap into, straight stitch 1/2" from the folded end using Sulky Polyester Invisible Thread.

2. Spray KK 2000 onto the back of a Velcro dot or patch and place it on the inside, pointed end of the tie. Stitch it in place with Sulky Polyester Invisible Thread. Spray KK 2000 onto the back of the matching Velcro dot or patch and position it on the outside of the tie to match the position of the other Velcro dot. Stitch.

Note: You could also use a metal or plastic snap.

5

MAKE THE STRAP:

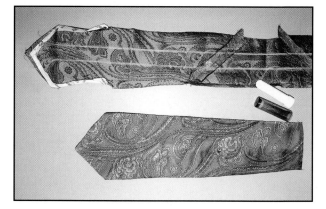

1. Tuck a 38" piece of rat tail cording into the channel on the narrow end. Edge stitch with Sulky Polyester Invisible Thread for 1/2", backstitch 1/2" catching the rat tail, then stitch forward to the bottom of the tie. Backstitch. Repeat on the left side.

2. On the outside, sew a small silk flower or button over the outline of the Velcro snap.

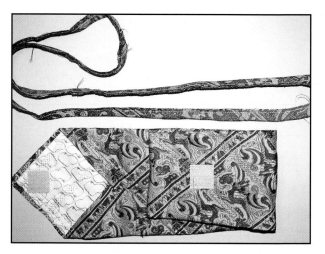

OPTIONAL:
TO MAKE A MATCHING STRAP FROM THE
REMAINDER OF THE TIE:

- Along the remaining end of the tie, clip the tack threads that hold the tie together.
- Remove the interfacing and cut away the silk facing at the point of the tie.
- Open and press.
- Draw a chalk line approximately 1/2" off center of the entire length of opened tie.
- From the drawn line, measure over 1" to the other side of the center and draw a second line.
- Accurately cut out this 1" wide piece with a rotary cutter and ruler to a length of 38" or length desired for strap.
- With right sides together, straight stitch a very scant 1/4" seam allowance. Trim the seam allowance.
- Turn right side out with a Fasturn tube turner. Since this remaining portion of the tie is bias, it turns easily without popping stitches, and likewise wears well as a strap.
- Insert and stitch down the strap as in #1 above.

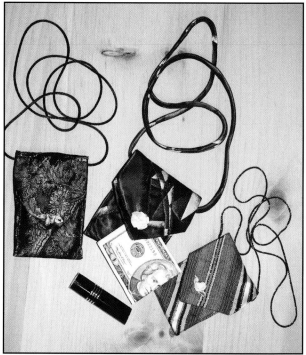

Patti's other assistant, Becky.

A Quick Quilted Project
Reversible Whole Cloth Vest

Designed and presented by
Joyce Drexler on the PBS TV Show
AMERICA SEWS
WITH SUE HAUSMANN

Photo by Frank Riemer

Joyce Drexler & Sue Hausmann
model Whole Cloth Vests on Sue's Program Set.

SUPPLIES:

- Your favorite Vest Pattern
  Joyce used: Sally Lampe's
  Long & Lean Vest Pattern
- Yardage that your vest pattern suggests
- Good Quality Sewing Thread
  for construction of vest
- Assorted types of Sulky Threads
- Sulky KK 2000 Temporary Spray Adhesive
  depending on technique you wish to use:
  Sulky Solvy Water Soluble Stabilizer
  Sulky Soft 'n Sheer Lightweight
  Permanent Stabilizer
- Twin Needle, Triple Needle
- Fleece

CUT OUT FABRIC YARDAGE:

1. Choose two fabrics that you simply love and want to wear. For ideas, look at the samples we used.

2. Lay the two fabrics, right sides together, on your cutting surface and lightly spray KK 2000 on the top layer. Remember to hold the can 6-10 inches away when spraying. We do not recommend spraying silk without a test first.

3. Lay your vest pattern pieces over it, smoothing them to the fabric. The KK 2000 will hold your pattern pieces without shifting for easy cutting with no pins.

4. Instead of cutting along the pattern line, add about 2" all around each pattern piece and rough cut to allow for "shrinkage" that might occur with quilting.

133

REVERSIBLE VEST ▶
EXAMPLE #1-A:
Each side of the vest was quilted separately.

Set Up Fabric:
- Top Layer   - Fabric *right side up*
- Middle Layer - Thin Fleece
- Bottom Layer- Sulky Soft 'n Sheer Stabilizer
  to prevent the fleece from getting caught in the throat plate hole of the machine while quilting.

Set Up Machine:
- **Use Twin Needle Spool Pins and two threads through 1 Size 14/90 Topstitch Needle**
  Place Sulky Ultra Twist #3045 on one spool pin and Sulky 30 wt. Rayon #1176 on the other spool pin.
- Loosen Top Tension slightly
- Bobbin Thread - Sulky Clear Invisible
- Lower Feed Dogs for Free-Motion
- Attach Darning Foot
- Select Straight Stitch
- Outline around the leaves and then stipple stitch around them to create relief for the leaves.

Fabric Credit: Benartex Fabrics

▲ REVERSIBLE VEST
EXAMPLE #1-B:
Each side of the vest was quilted separately.

Set Up Fabric:
- Top Layer   – Fabric *right side up*
- Middle Layer – Thin Fleece
- Bottom Layer – Sulky Soft 'n Sheer Stabilizer
  to prevent the fleece from getting caught in the throat plate hole of the machine while quilting.

Set Up Machine:

- Needle Thread - Sulky 40 wt. Variegated Rayon #2210
- Size 12/80 needle
- Loosen Top Tension slightly
- Bobbin Thread - Sulky Clear Invisible
- Lower Feed Dogs for Free-Motion
- Outline around the leaves and then stipple stitch around them to create relief for the leaves.

See page 139 for finishing the Vest.

REVERSIBLE VEST ▶
EXAMPLE #2-A:

Each side of the vest was quilted separately.

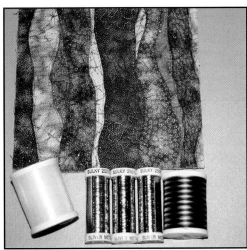

Set Up Fabric:
- Top Layer — Fabric *right side up*
- Middle Layer — Thin Fleece
- Bottom Layer — Sulky Soft 'n Sheer Stabilizer
  to prevent the fleece from getting caught in the throat plate hole of the machine while quilting.

Note: When using Sulky Sliver Metallic Thread, use it on a vertical spool pin.

Set Up Machine:
- **Use Twin Needle Vertical Spool Pins**
- **Use Twin Needle 3.0**
  Thread Sulky Sliver Metallic #8003 through one needle and Sulky Sliver Metallic #8053 through the other.
- Loosen Top Tension slightly,
  or for a more ridged look, tighten Top Tension
- Bobbin Thread - Sulky Clear Invisible
- Regular Presser Foot
- Feed Dogs Up
- Straight Stitch using about a 3.0 length

1. Twin needle stitch straddling the line separating each curved color change in the fabric.

2. Change to a single size 14/90 embroidery or topstitch needle, lower the feed dogs, and stipple stitch inside the aqua sections with Sulky Sliver #8053, inside the light green sections with Sulky Sliver #8003 and inside the medium green sections with Sulky Sliver #8024.

3. Thread up with Sulky 30 wt. Variegated Rayon #2131 and stipple stitch inside the dark green sections.

Fabric Credit: Hoffman Fabrics

▲ REVERSIBLE VEST
EXAMPLE #2-B:

Each side of the vest was quilted separately.

Set Up Fabric:
- Top Layer — Fabric *right side up*
- Middle Layer - Thin Fleece
- Bottom Layer - Sulky Soft 'n Sheer Stabilizer
  to prevent the fleece from getting caught in the throat plate hole of the machine while quilting.

Set Up Machine:
- 14/90 embroidery or topstitch needle
- Loosen Top Tension slightly
- Bobbin Thread - Sulky Clear Invisible
- Feed Dogs up
- Clear Straight Stitch Foot
- Straight Stitch using about a 3.0 length
- Sulky Sliver Metallic #8053
- Sulky 30 wt. Multi-Color #2246

Using Sulky Sliver Metallic #8053, stitch a wavy line on the green block print lines in the fabric. Then, lower the feed dogs, thread up with Sulky 30 wt. Multi-Color #2246, and stipple stitch between the block print lines.

See page 139 for finishing the Vest.

135

REVERSIBLE VEST ▶
EXAMPLE #3-A:

Each side of the vest was quilted separately.

Set Up Fabric:
• Top Layer – Fabric *right side up*
• Middle Layer – Thin Fleece
• Bottom Layer – Sulky Soft 'n Sheer Stabilizer
  *to prevent the fleece from getting
  caught in the throat plate hole of
  the machine while quilting.*

Set Up Machine:
• **Use Twin Needle Vertical Spool Pin**
• **Use Twin Needle 3.0**
  **Thread Sulky Sliver Metallic #8017 through
  one needle and Sulky Sliver Metallic #8024
  through the other needle.**
• **Loosen Top Tension slightly,**
  or for a more ridged look, tighten Top Tension
• Bobbin Thread - Sulky Clear Invisible
• Regular Presser Foot
• Feed Dogs Up
• Straight Stitch using about a 3.0 length

1. Twin needle stitch straddling the line separating
   each curved color change in the fabric.

2. Change to a single size 14/90 embroidery or
   topstitch needle, lower the feed dogs, and thread
   up with Sulky Metallic #7022 to stipple stitch or
   loosely fill-in wider, open areas.

Fabric Credit: Hoffman Fabrics

▲ REVERSIBLE VEST
EXAMPLE #3-B:

Each side of the vest was quilted separately.

Set Up Fabric:
• Top Layer – Fabric *right side up*
• Middle Layer – Thin Fleece
• Bottom Layer – Sulky Soft 'n Sheer Stabilizer
  *to prevent the fleece from getting
  caught in the throat plate hole of
  the machine while quilting.*

Set Up Machine:
• 14/90 Metallic Needle
• Loosen Top Tension slightly
• Bobbin Thread - Sulky Clear Invisible
• Feed Dogs down
• Darning Foot or fabric in a hoop
• Sulky Sliver Opalescent Metallic #8040

Using Sulky Sliver #8040, free-motion straight stitch
following the design in the fabric. The Opalescent
Thread picks up whatever color or shade it crosses in
the print and beautifully reflects that color.

See page 139 for finishing the Vest.

REVERSIBLE VEST ▶
EXAMPLE #4-A:

Each side of the vest was quilted separately.

Set Up Fabric:
- Top Layer   – Fabric *right side up*
- Middle Layer – Thin Fleece
- Bottom Layer – Sulky Soft 'n Sheer Stabilizer
  to prevent the fleece from getting caught in the throat plate hole of the machine while quilting.

Set Up Machine:
- **Use Twin Needle Vertical Spool Pins**
- **Use Twin Needle 3.0**
  Thread Sulky Sliver Metallic #8016 through one of the needles and Sulky Sliver #8012 through the other.
- Loosen Top Tension slightly,
  or for a more ridged look, tighten Top Tension.
- Bobbin Thread - Sulky Clear Invisible
- Regular Presser Foot
- Feed Dogs Up
- Straight Stitch using about a 3.0 length

1. Twin needle stitch straddling the line separating each curved color change in the fabric.

2. Change to a single size 14/90 embroidery or topstitch needle, lower the feed dogs, and stipple stitch inside the purple sections with Sulky Sliver Metallic #8012 and over the blue sections with Sulky Sliver #8016.

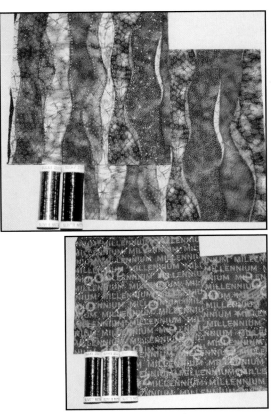

Fabric Credits: Hoffman and RJR Fabrics

▲ REVERSIBLE MILLENNIUM
VEST EXAMPLE #4-B:

Each side of the vest was quilted separately.

Set Up Fabric:
- Top Layer   – Fabric *right side up*
- Middle Layer – Thin Fleece
- Bottom Layer – Sulky Soft 'n Sheer Stabilizer
  to prevent the fleece from getting caught in the throat plate hole of the machine while quilting.

Set Up Machine:
- 3.0 Triple Needle
- Loosen Top Tension slightly
- Bobbin Thread - Sulky Clear Invisible
- Feed Dogs Up
- Clear Zig-Zag Foot and Quilting Guide for Crosshatch Quilting
- Sulky Sliver Metallic #8052 in the left needle, #8001 in the center needle, and #8016 in the right needle.

Stitch a 1" crosshatch by first drawing a diagonal line with chalk as a beginning guide. Do the same to stitch the opposite direction. Crosshatch the entire vest. The middle Sulky Sliver sits right on top of this stitching ridge, giving a very dramatic look to simple crosshatching.

See page 139 for finishing the Vest.

REVERSIBLE VEST
EXAMPLE #5-A: ▶

Set Up Fabric:
- Top Layer   – Fabric *right side up*
- Bottom Layer – 2nd Fabric *right side down*

No batting was used in this vest. It was stabilized by laying Solvy on one layer of the vest, spritzing the Solvy with water, laying the other vest layer on top, and ironing the two layers together; both sides were then quilted at the same time.

Set Up Machine:
- **Vertical Spool Pins**
- 14/90 or 16/100 Embroidery Needle
- Bobbin Thread - Sulky Multi-Color 30 wt. Rayon #2245
- Thread the top with **2 spools** of Sulky 30 wt. Rayon #1176 **through the same needle**
- Loosen Top Tension slightly
- Feed Dogs Down
- Darning Foot or fabric in a hoop

In the botanical print fabric, free-motion outline stitch either around the leaves or the box-like areas, or whatever pleases you. As you stitch the top side, the bobbin thread is being applied to the lining fabric (reverse side of vest). With this method, you must bind the vest to finish it.

▲ REVERSIBLE METALLIC VEST
EXAMPLE #6-A:

by Dian Keepers

Set Up Fabric:
- Top Layer   – Fabric *right side up*
- Bottom Layer – Fabric *right side down*

Note: This was done on a professional long-arm machine, but you could duplicate the stitching on your machine.

Set Up Machine:
- 14/90 Metallic Needle
- Loosen Top Tension slightly
- Needle Thread - Sulky Sliver Metallic #8001 on a vertical spool pin
- Bobbin Thread - Sulky Metallic #7001
- Feed Dogs Down
- Darning Foot or fabric in a hoop

Following the flow of the print, Dian free-motion quilted the entire vest with Sliver on one side and Metallic Thread on the other at the same time.

138

FAUX APPLIQUE:

Fabrics like these are perfect for this technique because the designs are clean and have lots of background color surrounding them. It's easy to make them look appliqued. The Cats were outlined with a "feather stitch".

You could also use a Blanket Stitch and Sulky 30 wt. #1005 Black for the look of Hand Applique, or simply Outline Stitch them with a straight stitch, first with one color of Sulky Sliver and then again with a second color of Sliver for a flashier look.

To the right are some other fabrics that would be great for Faux Applique.

FINISHING THE VESTS:

1. On all vests except #5-A and #6-A, layer the two quilted/embellished vest pieces together, wrong sides together, with the Soft 'n Sheer Stabilizer still in place; place the Vest pattern piece on top.

Spray KK 2000 on the layers and pattern pieces to keep them from shifting.

2. Cut through all layers with a rotary cutter following the Vest pattern lines.

3. All the Vests except #5-A and #6-A can be sewn using basic directions for a reversible Vest.

4. For Vest #5-A or #6-A, you must bind the raw edges. (See page 160 for French Fold binding directions.)

CONSTRUCTION:

1. Sew together shoulder seams of inside Vest fronts and inside Vest back. Repeat for outer Vest fronts and Vest back. With right sides together, sew inner Vest to outer Vest around the arm holes, neck front and bottom of the Vest. DO NOT SEW SIDE SEAMS. To make seams lay flatter, clip curved areas with sharp scissors or cut seam allowance with pinking shears or rotary pinking blade.

2. Turn the vest right side out by pulling Vest back through the shoulder and out the Vest front side opening. Pull points out with a pin to make them fully turned out. Press edges completely.

3. Carefully match Vest side seams; sew them together as much as you can on the machine, then Hand Slip-Stitch the remainder of the opening closed. Press side seams.

4. Edge stitch around the entire Vest using the edge foot and a Sulky Decorative Thread in the bobbin that matches the side of the Vest on the bottom and a top thread that matches the Vest that is right side up as you stitch.

139

A Quick Quilted Project
Odds & Ends Purse

Designed by Ellen Osten
Presented by Joyce Drexler
on the PBS TV Show SEW CREATIVE

1

SUPPLIES:

- Scraps of Assorted Fabrics or 1/2 yd. of 45" fabric
- 1/2 yd. Fleece or Lightweight Batting
- 1/2 yd. decorative cording for purse strap
- 1 package Sulky Tear-Easy Stabilizer
- Sulky KK 2000 Temporary Spray Adhesive
- All Purpose Sewing Thread to match fabrics
- Assorted Sulky Threads
- Machine Sewing Needles: Size 12/80 and Size 14/90 Embroidery or Quilting Needles
- Large Sew-in Snap
- Scissors, Ruler & Mat, Rotary Cutter
- Marking Pen
- Pins

2

PREPARE FABRIC PIECES:

1. Using the entire purse pattern (found on pull-out pattern sheet), cut one each of:
   fashion fabric lining
   (coordinating fabric) fleece.

2. Use your fashion fabric or make the fabric for a front purse pocket by piecing together several scraps of contrasting fabrics. Press. Then cut out the front pocket from that fabric as well as fleece and lining, using the front-pocket cutting line on the purse pattern.

Cut the optional back pocket from the fashion fabric or a contrasting fabric using the back-pocket cutting line on the purse pattern.

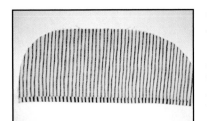

Ellen Osten
St. Petersburg, FL

Ellen has been teaching professionally for over 25 years and has been a part of Speed Stitch/Sulky of America since 1988. She taught at several of the S.M.A.R.T. (Speed Stitch Machine Arts Retreat) events before becoming a Sulky Educator, teaching all of the "Sew Exciting Seminars". She is published in several of the "Concepts in Sulky" books. She also teaches sit and sew classes in tailoring, fitting, free-motion embroidery, expert cutwork, plus many other techniques.

When she is at home, she continues to run "Creative Sewing", a custom sewing and tailoring business, and "Sew What's New", a line of her patterns. This enabled her to be at home raising five children, who are all grown now, and have blessed her with nine grandchildren.

So now it's Grammie (Ellen) and her constant companion, Cricket, a Brussels Griffon. Ellen says, "she likes to sleep on top of my feet when I'm sewing, and best of all...she loves me no matter what I weigh!"

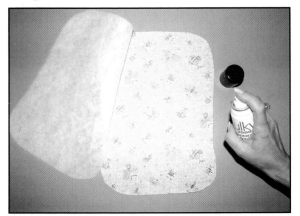

3. Spray the wrong side of the main purse fabric with KK 2000 and place the fleece on it. To keep fabric from puckering, place one or two layers of Tear-Easy underneath any embroidery area. Use your favorite Sulky Threads to do decorative stitching or embroidery to highlight the fabric.

CONSTRUCT THE PURSE:

1. The optional back pocket: On the top edge, turn the fabric under 1/4" and top-stitch along folded edge.

2. The front pocket: Make a sandwich: Fleece on the bottom, front pocket fabric right side up, and lining wrong side up. Stitch a seam 1/4" from the edge across the top (straight edge). To keep the seam from rolling to the right side, fold open just the lining, then straight stitch through the lining and seam allowance about 1/8" from the seam. Fold the lining closed at the first seam and press.

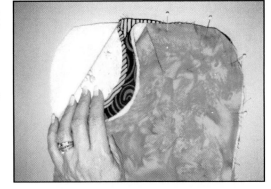

3. The purse: Lay the fleece down first, place the purse fabric right side up over the fleece, and position the optional back pocket on top with the wrong side of the pocket to the right side of the purse. Pin or spray with KK 2000 as you go.

4. Lay the front pocket unit with the right side of the fashion or pieced fabric down against the right side of the back pocket, and the right side of the lining facing up; match all of the cut edges.

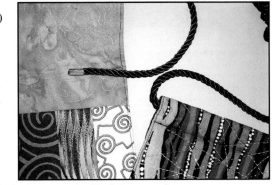

5. Lay purse lining right side down on top of the whole sandwich. Pin. Sew all layers together around outside edge with a 1/4" seam allowance, leaving a 4" opening to turn through to the right side. Clip and notch curves. Turn right side out. Press. Topstitch with a Sulky Decorative Thread all the way around, which closes the opening at the same time. Fold flap down. There should be about one inch between the top of the front pocket and the fold of the flap. Press folded flap edge. Open out. Lay cut ends of cords on top of the press line. Stitch through cord several times, then fold flap back in place. Topstitch with a Sulky Decorative Thread 3/4" from the top of fold.

6. To help keep the purse closed, sew a snap in place. Add any extra buttons, pins and/or beads to enhance your purse.

141

A Quick Quilted Project

Embellished Photo Mats

Designed by Ellen Osten

1

SUPPLIES:

- Zig-zag Sewing Machine and Attachments (Embroidery unit optional)
- Open-Toe Applique Foot
- Free-Motion Embroidery Foot
- 11" x 14" Picture Frame with 8" x 10" mat opening
- 14" x 16" Background Fabric
- 1/4 yd. or fat quarter of contrast fabric for letters
- 1/4 yd. Steam-A-Seam 2
- 1 Pkg. Sulky Tear-Easy Stabilizer
- 1 Pkg. Sulky Totally Stable Iron-On Stabilizer
- Sulky KK 2000 Temporary Spray Adhesive
- An Assortment of Decorative Sulky Threads
- Sulky Polyester Bobbin Thread
- Embroidery or Topstitch Needle Size 14/90
- Sharp, Pointed Scissors
- Seam Sealant (Fray Check or Stop Fray)
- Permanent-Ink, Fine-Line Marker
- Temporary Fabric Marker
- Happy Birthday Letters on pull-out pattern sheet
- New Home Memory Card #19 - Wild Animal Series

2

PREPARE FABRIC PIECES:

1. Use picture frame for size and letter placement. Using a Temporary Fabric Marker, trace mat opening onto the right side of the background fabric.

2. Trace the already reversed letters onto one side of Steam-A-Seam 2. Cut them out and fuse them onto the wrong side of the contrast fabric. Cut the letters out of the fabric. Remove paper backing. Using the mat line as your guide, slightly overlap the letters as you lay them on the right side of the background fabric.

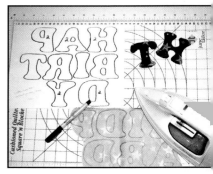

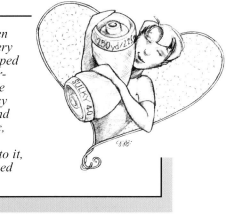

Hint: When Ellen did the embroidery designs, she hooped one layer of Tear-Easy, sprayed the hooped Tear-Easy with KK 2000 and placed the fabric, with the Totally Stable ironed onto it, against the hooped Tear-Easy.

Follow manufacturer's directions for fusing.

3. Iron two layers of Totally Stable to the back of the fabric, extending two to three inches from the edges of the fabric.

3

EMBROIDER AND QUILT:

1. If you are doing computerized embroidery, thread your machine with Sulky Decorative Thread on the top and Sulky Polyester Bobbin Thread in the bobbin, follow your machine set-up instructions, and proceed with placement of embroidery. You can also do free-motion embroidery (Thread Painting). Refer to the book "Embroidery Concepts in Sulky" if you need help with Thread Painting.

2. After embroidering is complete, apply a seam sealant such as Fray Check on all the embroidered edges. Let dry. Remove Tear-Easy from back. To trim away all of the **background fabric only** from the center, using sharp, pointed scissors, poke the scissor point **under the fabric only**; clip the fabric enough so that you can slip your finger under it to gently lift it away from the Totally Stable and trim it very close to the embroidery designs and letters. **Do not tear or cut Totally Stable.**

4

CONSTRUCT THE MAT:

1. Re-press Totally Stable in place if any of it has become unattached to the fabric due to the excessive handling.

2. Set up machine for Applique: Attach the open-toe foot; raise the feed dogs; set the machine for a 3.0 width zig-zag; set the length for a close satin stitch. Loosen upper tension two or three notches. (The "Applique Concepts in Sulky" Book is a good refresher book if you need help.) Satin stitch around the letters. Blend the satin stitch into the embroidery designs. Remove the stabilizer. By stitching with your stitch length very close, the stabilizer should perforate well, allowing it to tear away very cleanly.

Extra touch: To add a beautiful sparkle, straight stitch Sulky Sliver Metallic, with a 1.5 length, next to the satin stitching in the inside of the letter.

3. Spray the frame mat with KK 2000. Lay the wrong side of the fabric on top of the mat. Turn it over and spray the back of the mat. Lay your favorite picture in place. You should be looking at the back of the photo. Trim excess fabric even with the edge of the mat. Put into the picture frame and replace the backing.

4. Sign and date. Wonderful for all special events: anniversaries, graduations, holidays, etc.!

143

A Quick Quilted Project
Stationery Keeper

Designed by Ellen Osten

Finished Size: 12" x 19" (when open)

Presented by Joyce Drexler on the PBS TV Show
SEW CREATIVE with Donna Wilder

SUPPLIES:

- Fabric: 20" x 45"
- Thin Batting: 12" x 20"
- Sulky KK 2000 Temporary Spray Adhesive
- 1 package each:
  Sulky Cut-Away Plus
  Sulky Tear-Easy
  Sulky Solvy (if doing computerized embroidery)
- 20" of 1/2" wide ribbon
- All purpose Sewing Thread
- Assorted Sulky Decorative Threads
- 80/12 Sewing Machine Needle.
- Embroidery or Top-stitch Needle Size 90/14
- Ruler, Rotary Cutter and Mat
- Chalk Marker
- Pins • Scissors

PREPARE FABRIC PIECES:

1. Choose a fabric with an all-over design.
*(Important note about fabric choices: The fabric needs to be 45"
wide with selvages that are 1/2" or less. Slightly narrower fabric
will result in less height, limiting your choice of paper pads or
stationery; or you could make your pocket depths smaller. One-way
designs do not work well.)*
Do not cut off selvages.

2. Fold fabric in half lengthwise and crease (or use the
crease that comes in the fabric as purchased on the bolt).
Open fabric wrong side up and spray KK 2000 from the
crease 12" out to the right.

3. Spread the 12" x 20" batting on top of the sprayed fabric
next to the crease. To prevent the fabric sandwich from
shifting and puckering, spray KK 2000 on a layer of Tear-
Easy and place it over the batting (see photo on next page).

144

EMBELLISH AND QUILT:

1. See diagram for placement of embellishment. Use decorative stitches, embroidery designs and/or free-motion stippling to embellish to your heart's content with Sulky Decorative Threads. Add additional stabilizer as needed. *Try using one of Joyce Drexler's Inspirational Concepts in Sulky Embroidery Designs from Amazing Designs.*

CONSTRUCT THE KEEPER:

1. Cut a 10-1/2" x 20" piece of Sulky Cut-Away Plus and place it adjacent to the batting so that edges will touch the batting or slightly overlap it. Fold the fabric so the right sides and selvage edges are together. Use a 1/2" seam allowance to sew selvage edges together, catching Cut-Away Plus in the seam allowance.

2. Turn right side out. Press seam. Place decorative side down and smooth fabric so that everything is laying nicely. To make the upper pockets, fold the seam edge up so that it is laying parallel to the folded edge about 8" from the top. Press. The next fold for the lower pockets is just above the bottom seam edge about 10" down from the top. Press. Feeling the edge of the batting through all layers will help you to keep everything even. Pin through the fabric and the Cut-Away Plus layers only, leaving sides free for turning to the wrong side.

3. Place the ribbon ties on the 12" sides, centered and even with the cut edge; pin or baste in position, again through fabric and Cut-Away Plus layers only.

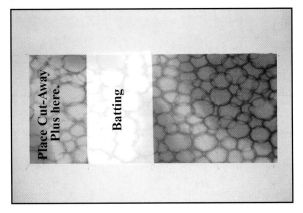

Place Cut-Away Plus here.

Batting

Placement for Embroidery

45"

center crease | Top of Design ← | front

center | back

20"

4. Carefully turn entire project wrong side out, spray KK 2000 on another 10-1/2" x 20" piece of Cut-Away Plus, and lay it on the wrong side of the fabric, not the batting side. Tuck ribbons inside the sandwich. Use a 1/4" to 3/8" seam allowance to sew both ends closed, catching the Cut-Away Plus edges in the stitching. Leave a 3" opening on one end to turn the project right side out; turn and lay flat. Make sure pockets are still in place.

5. Choose a Sulky Decorative Thread to topstitch about 1/8" from the edge all the way around the outside edge. This will close the opening at the same time. Topstitch the pockets.

6. On the inside of the Stationery Keeper, find the center width. Mark it from top to bottom with a chalk marker. Stitch 1/4" to the right of this mark and 3/4" to the left of this mark. This makes a 1" channel for pens and allows the Stationery Keeper to fold properly. To divide the pockets into two or four sections, stitch a seam from the bottom to the pocket top edge on one or both sides.

145

A Quick Quilted Project
Window to the Millennium

Designed, Pieced and Quilted by Ellen Osten   Approx. 37" x 37"

1

SUPPLIES:

- Millennium Fabric by Fabric Traditions
- 1/2 yd. Fairfield Low-Loft Batting
- Sulky KK 2000 Temporary Spray Adhesive
- All Purpose Sewing Thread to match fabrics
- Sulky Sliver Metallic Thread #8001, #8014 and #8016
- Sulky Smoke Invisible Thread
- Machine Sewing Needles: Size 80/12 and Size 90/14 Embroidery or Quilting Needles
- Scissors, Ruler & Mat, Rotary Cutter
- Marking Pen
- Pins

2

PREPARE FABRIC PIECES:

- "Fussy Cut" (see page #48) nine 6-1/2" squares from Building Motif Millennium Fabric
- Cut six 1-1/2" x 8-1/2" strips of Red 2000 Fabric
  Cut six 1-1/2" x 30" strips of Red 2000 Fabric
- Cut nine 2-1/2" x 6-1/2" strips of White 2000 Fabric
- Cut nine 2-1/2" x 6-1/2" strips of Blue 2000 Fabric
- Cut four 5-1/2" x 38" strips of Sparkling Blue 2000 for Border
- Cut four 2-1/2" x 38" strips of Sparkling Blue for Binding
- Use 2" Finished Triangle Paper and the White and Blue 2000 Fabric to make the Half-Square Triangles which are used to make the angles in the blocks. (See pages 34-35.)

Use a 1/4" seam allowance throughout.

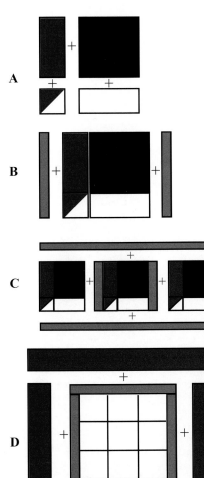

A

B

C

D

1. Add a 2-1/2" x 6-1/2" strip of white 2000 Fabric to the 6-1/2" square of the Building Print (Illustration "A"). Press.
2. Add a half-square triangle to the end of the 2-1/2" x 6-1/2" blue 2000 Fabric strip. Press. Join both units together to make an 8-1/2" square block (Illustration "A"). Press.
3. Create 9 of these blocks. Make 1 more for a pillow, if desired. Arrange the building prints in the order in which you want them to appear in the quilt.
4. Determine your three vertical center blocks and add a 1-1/2" x 8-1/2" Red 2000 strip to each vertical side of all three blocks (Illustration "B"). Press.
5. Attach one block to either side of the 3 vertical center blocks (Illustration "C"), being mindful of the placement you determined in #3. Press.
6. Add a 1-1/2" red sashing strip to the top and bottom of the horizontal center row of blocks (Illustration "C"). Then, attach the top and bottom rows of blocks to this red sashing strip. Press.
7. Add a 1-1/2" red sashing strip to both sides of the 9-block unit, then to the top and bottom of the unit.
8. To make your "quilt sandwich" see page 69.

For Finishing - See pages 157-160.

9. Add Border Fabric, applying straight-cut corners (Illustration "D").
10. Stitch in the ditch (see page 10) around each block and the sashing strips using Sulky Smoke Invisible Thread.
11. Quilt each block by stitching three parallel rows 1/2" apart on the white and blue accent strips using Sulky Sliver starting with color #8014, followed by #8001, and then #8016.
12. Using the quilting template that decorates page 146, trace the design with a permanent-ink marker onto Sulky Solvy. Spray KK 2000 onto the quilt border area and strategically place the stars where you want them to fall. (Notice that Ellen overlapped some of the large stars onto the red sashing area.) To remove the Solvy without submerging the quilt in water, run a wet Q-Tip along the stitching line and the Solvy will pull away easily.
13. Add the Hanging Sleeve.
14. Add the Binding.

First Grade Snow Days through Mom's Window

Designed, Pieced and Quilted by Marilyn Fisher

This Alexander Henry Fabric Collection reminded Marilyn of the grade school snow days she loved as a child. Her mom always let her play in the snow. Building snowmen, skating on the pond behind the house, and sliding down hills not far from the house would make for great fun!

Quilted with Sulky Sliver Metallic Thread that adds to the icy feeling of the print.

Finished Size 36" x 45"   **147**

A Quick Quilted Project
Embroidered Landscape

Designed by Patsy Shields

Finished size:11-1/4" H x 12-1/4" W without borders

1
SUPPLIES:

- 12" x 13" piece of Muslin for foundation
- 6 fat quarters of assorted fabrics in nature colors.
  4 - 3" x 18" strips for Borders
- Sulky Rayon Thread (In 40 wt. Patsy used: #1176 and #2243; in Ultra Twist #3034 and #3025).
- Sulky Polyester Bobbin Thread
- Sulky Invisible Polyester Thread
- Sulky Tear-Easy Stabilizer
- Sulky KK 2000 Temporary Spray Adhesive
- Sulky Solvy Stabilizer
- Embroidery Hoop

2
CREATE FABRIC PIECES:

1. To scrunch up the tree and lower left ground fabric, wet it, smush it, and press the scrunch in with a hot iron until dry. Iron fusible interfacing onto the back of each piece. Set aside for now.

2. To make dimensional leaves, use a fusible web to fuse together enough leaf fabric to cut out two leaves. Use KK 2000 to hold them in place between two layers of Solvy; secure in an embroidery hoop. Thread the top and bobbin with Sulky #1176 and satin stitch around the leaves. Remove the Solvy and set aside.

3. Spray KK 2000 on the back of the sky fabric and place it on the muslin. Continue spraying and placing each consecutive fabric below the previous one, overlapping about 1/4".

Patsy Shields

National Director of
Education for Sulky of America

Patsy has traveled extensively throughout the U.S. for over 15 years as a free-lance sewing specialist teaching serger classes, fitting workshops, and machine art seminars.

She has been published in the *Serger Update Newsletter* and has contributed to a book for the *Singer Reference Library*, to *Sew News* and the *Patchwork Concepts in Sulky Book* as well as co-authoring the *Updated Serger Concepts in Sulky Book*.

She has taught at National Sewing Events including *S.M.A.R.T., Baby Lock Tech, New Home Institute, Quilt Market and Quilt Festival* as well as *Sulky Instructor Training Seminars* and over a hundred *Sulky "Sew Exciting" Seminars*.

As National Director of Education for Sulky of America, she coordinates Sulky's Educational Activity at trade shows and consumer shows as well as training Sulky Free-Lance Educators to conduct *"Sew Exciting Seminars"*.

◀ 4. Hill

◀ 5. Ground ▶

EMBELLISH WITH STITCHING:

1. Spray KK 2000 on each of two layers of Tear-Easy and place them under the landscape-covered muslin.

2. Attach the applique foot and begin stitching down the fabric layers with decorative stitches, changing the Sulky thread colors as necessary. If another fabric overlaps, move it out of the way so the stitches can go below it, then smooth it back in place. Patsy frayed a 6" strip of woven fabric and tucked it into a pleat of the ground fabric to add dimension and interest.

3. Attach the darning foot, lower the feed dogs and thread up with Sulky Ultra Twist #3034. Free-motion straight stitch some trees on the top hills. Refer to the picture for the shape. Change to green Ultra Twist #3025 and make free-motion circles to form bushes between the trees.

4. Raise the feed dogs, attach the applique foot and create a fence on the top left hill by sewing small satin stitches about 1/2" long and about 5/8" apart for the "rails". With a three-step or regular straight stitch, stitch a line just below the top of the rails.

5. Draw the tree shape on the fusible web and fuse it to the interfaced side of the scrunched tree fabric. Cut out the tree, turn under the edges about 1/4", then fuse it onto the left side of the landscape picture about 1" to 1-1/2" from the edge.

6. Cut the scrunched **ground** fabric so that it covers the edge of the tree; turn under the edges, and place it on the picture with narrow strips of fusible web under the top edges. **Do not fuse yet.**

7. Draw the other 3 leaves on the fusible web and iron it onto the wrong side of the leaf fabric. Cut out the leaves and fuse 2 of them onto the landscape just under the hill fabric. Satin stitch around the edges with Sulky #1176.

8. Tuck the two dimensional leaves under the scrunched ground fabric. Straight stitch the hill fabric in place, keeping the dimensional leaves out of the way but catching the bottom edges in the stitching. Place the 3rd leaf to overlap the hill fabric; fuse the leaf and ground fabric in place. Tack down each dimensional leaf on one of its points.

9. Add flowers and satin-stitched leaves to fill in the picture. Refer to the picture for placement. Make the tall stems with either a wavy or straight line of satin stitches. Add flowers on either side of the stem using machine flower designs or free-motion shapes. Vary the Sulky 40 wt. thread colors for the different flowers. Add small flowers on the second hill beside the tree and the satin stitched leaves.

◀ 3. Hill

10. Use Sulky Multi-Color #2243 to stitch some flower shapes on or beside the stems, using either a star stitch or any stitch you have that looks like a flower. Or, you can create flowers with a zig-zag stitch by setting the machine for a wide zig-zag, lowering the feed dogs, stitching in place several times, then rotating the fabric slightly and repeating. Have the stitch start on the inside (left) and stop on the left before you pivot the fabric. Make several "petals" until you have a circular shape that looks like a star. Vary the width of the zig-zag to vary the size of the flowers.

◀

4. Ground

Make "fuzzy" flowers by placing scissors under the threads of the "petal" as close to the outside as possible. Clip. Brush with your fingers to "fuzz".

11. To simulate bark, use Ultra Twist #3034 to add some straight stitching to the length of the big scrunched tree; also stitch over the scrunched bottom ground fabric to hold it in place.

◀ 6.

12. Remove the stabilizer from the back. Straighten the edges of the picture with a ruler and a rotary cutter. Add a 3" border to the outside edges. Follow quilting preparation instructions on page 69, and binding instructions on pages 160.

Foreground

149

A Quick Quilted Project
The Garden Gate

Designed and presented by Joyce Drexler on the PBS TV Show **AMERICA SEWS WITH SUE HAUSMANN**

Sue's husband, Herb, digitized a similar design in the Husqvarna Viking customizing system. You can find this FREE digitized pattern of the Garden Gate on the Husqvarna Viking website: www.husqvarna viking.com

1

THREAD TIP:

When winding Invisible Thread on a plastic bobbin, always wind slowly to avoid breaking it.

SUPPLIES:

- 10" German Wooden Machine Embroidery Hoop
- 1 – 15" square of woven fabric
- 1 – 6" square of white poly-blend fabric for photo transfer
- Bunnies are from Noah's Ark I, Cactus Punch Embroidery Card designed by Carol Ingram
- 3 – 15" squares of Sulky Tear-Easy Stabilizer
- 3 – 15" squares of Sulky Super Solvy Stabilizer
- 1 – 7" x 9" piece of Sulky Sticky Stabilizer
- Sulky Threads– See Color Key on next page
- Sulky Premium Clear Invisible Thread in Bobbin
- Sulky KK 2000 Temporary Spray Adhesive

If making a pillow (use photo as guide):
- 12" Pillow Form
- 2 – 12" x 15" Fabric Squares for back of Pillow
- 2 yds. of Cording
- 2 – 1-1/2" x 45" strips of mottled fabric to match flower color
- 2 – 3" x 45" strips of small green print for borders
- Sewing Thread for construction of Pillow

INSTRUCTIONS TO "FREE-MOTION" EMBROIDER THE DESIGN:

Do the following unless you elect to scan the design and digitize it for computerized embroidery:

1. Spray Sulky KK 2000 onto the Garden Gate pattern (found on the pull-out pattern sheet).

2. Smooth a 15" square of Super Solvy over the pattern with the pattern centered in the middle of the Super Solvy; trace the pattern onto the Solvy with a permanent-ink marker.

3. Spray KK 2000 onto the 15" square of woven fabric that you wish to embroider and smooth the Solvy Gate Pattern onto it.

4. Spray KK 2000 onto the back of the woven square of fabric and smooth a 15" square of Tear-Easy onto it. Repeat with another layer of Tear-Easy that has the grain running in the same direction as the first piece. Add a third piece of Tear-Easy, but with the grain flowing in the opposite direction.

5. Secure in a 10" wooden machine embroidery hoop. Be sure all layers are smooth and that the grain of the fabric has not been distorted. The fabric must be tight as a drum in the hoop.

6. Set up your machine for Free-motion Embroidery:

   • Lower Feed Dogs
   • Put a new 14/90 Embroidery or Topstitch Needle in Machine
   • Lower Top Tension
   • Bobbin - Sulky Clear Polyester Invisible Thread

7. Embroider following the Color Key and Stitching Key on this page.

If you want detailed help in learning how to do free-motion embroidery, consult the "Embroidery Concepts in Sulky" Book 900B-10.

IF USING THE NOAH'S ARK EMBROIDERY CARD TO STITCH OUT THE BUNNIES:

If you wish to use the Cactus Punch Card to embroider the Bunnies, remove the fabric from the hoop and tear away the Tear-Easy. Secure 1 layer of Sulky Sticky behind the outer ring of the Computerized Machine Embroidery hoop. Position the Embroidered Gate on top of the Sticky. You do not need to use the inner hoop.

Color Key

Gate - Sulky Ultra Twist #3022
Photo Frame - Sulky Ultra Twist #3018
Posts - Sulky Ultra Twist #3037
Flowers - Sulky Ultra Twist #3031
Green Vines & Leaves
   - Sulky Ultra Twist #3027
Outline - Sulky Ultra Twist #3019

Bunnies -
Use Sulky 40 wt. Rayon
Colors as indicated on
Noah's Ark I Embroidery Card
or substitute some Sulky Ultra Twist
for added texture and dimension.

Sugg.	We used	Sugg.	We used
1011	1219	1005	1005
1219	3022	1117	1117
1041	3007	1147	1039
1001	1001	1051	3027
		1049	3041

Stitching Key

Gate - Satin/Fill-in Stitch
Posts - Side Stitch Fill-in
Flowers - Tapered Satin Stitch
   or Side Stitch Fill-In,
   or substitute Silk Ribbon
Green Vines & Leaves
   Straight Stitch and
   Straight Stitch Fill-in
Outline - Straight Stitch
Bunnies - *COMPUTERIZED*
   EMBROIDERY
   or free-motion
   side stitch fill-in

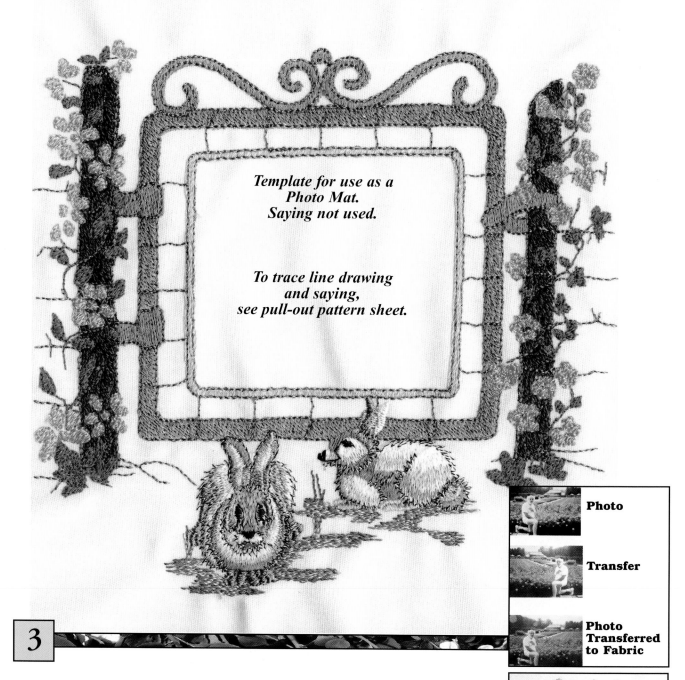

*Template for use as a
Photo Mat.
Saying not used.*

*To trace line drawing
and saying,
see pull-out pattern sheet.*

Photo

Transfer

Photo
Transferred
to Fabric

3

INSTRUCTION FOR PHOTO MAT:

1. Take a favorite photo (that will fit in the window opening above) to a Quick Print or Kinko's and have them make an iron-on transfer of the photo and transfer it onto a 6" square of white poly-blend fabric.
2. Once the gate design is completely embroidered and the excess stabilizer is trimmed away, carefully cut away the photo mat template fabric up to the satin stitching.
3. Spray the back of the Embroidered Mat with Sulky KK 2000 and center the transferred photo fabric under the embroidered mat.
4. Center the embroidered mat between two layers of Sulky Super Solvy and re-hoop.
5. Stitch another slightly wider satin stitch over the previous row of narrow satin stitching, allowing the needle to swing over the cut edge to finish it.
6. Trim away excess photo fabric. Tear away Super Solvy from the front and back.
7. Use as a quilt block, pillow or framed photo mat.

A Quick Quilted Project
Fabric Tissue Box Cover

Designed by Ethel Bedford

This is a wonderful way to use up your quilting scraps. It takes just a few minutes to make, and presto! - you've got a tissue box that matches the beautiful quilt that you just made. They're so quick and easy, you could make one for every holiday by just using different holiday fabrics. If you have computerized machine embroidery capability, it's a wonderful way to showcase your designs.

1

SUPPLIES:

- 16" x 19" piece of fabric
  If quilting the fabric, use a larger piece of fabric and cut it down to 16" x 20" after quilting.
- 24" piece of ribbon
- Sulky 30 wt. Rayon Thread, matching or decorative for casing
- Good quality Sewing Thread
- Fray Check™ (optional)

Optional embroidery:
- Sulky 40 wt. Rayon Threads
- 9" square of Totally Stable
- 9" square of Sulky Tear-Easy
- Amazing Designs Embroidery Card #AD3000 "Inspirational Concepts in Sulky" Designed by Joyce Drexler; or "Winter Scenes" #23 designed by Carol Ingram for Cactus Punch.

2

INSTRUCTIONS:

Embroidery Note: If you do not wish to add an embroidery, go to Step 2.

1. Iron a 9" square of Totally Stable onto the wrong side of the 16" high x 19" wide fabric, 2" from the bottom and in the center. Mark placement of design. (Ethel placed her 3" high tree design 5" from the bottom and 9" from the side which was the middle of a 4" hoop.) Hoop fabric with Sulky Tear-Easy Stabilizer underneath, and embroider your chosen design with Sulky 40 wt. Rayon Threads. Remove stabilizers.

Note: To use a larger design, like one of Joyce's Inspirational Concepts in Sulky Designs which are about 4" square, position the bottom of the design about 3" from the bottom of the 16" x 19" fabric.

2. Clean-finish only the top by turning it under 1/4" and stitching it down.

3. Fold it lengthwise, right sides together, and sew the lengthwise edges together. Then sew the bottom raw edges together.

4. Turn down the top edge 3", wrong sides together, press, and then sew along the clean-finished edge with a zig-zag or straight stitch using Sulky 30 wt. Rayon Thread. To form the casing, measure up 1" from this stitching, mark with a chalk marker, and then straight stitch across it. Measure up 1/2" from this stitched line and add another straight stitched line.

5. To make contoured corners, with wrong sides together, fold the top edge in half lengthwise and bar-tack at the open end (not the top, folded end) in the seam allowance.

6. Turn right side out. Using your seam line as the center back, mark the center front point in the casing. Carefully cut a small hole in the first layer of fabric only. Do not cut through the second fabric. Apply Fray Check, if desired. When it is dry, insert the ribbon. Place a tissue box inside, draw up the ribbon, and make a bow. What a quick gift to make.

A Quick Quilted Project
A Puffy Foam Welcome

Finished
size
4" x 18"

Patti Jo Larson
Viking Educator
from Sheyenne, ND

*Patti Jo is a regular on the PBS TV program
"American Sews with Sue Hausmann". As a
traveling Education Consultant for Viking, she loves
inspiring others to be creative with their sewing skills.
Specializing in heirloom sewing and working
with French Hand Sewing experts,
Martha Pullen and Kathy McMakin,
she has brought Traveling Schools of
Art Fashion across the United States.*

1

SUPPLIES:

- 9" x 24" Striped
  Decorator Fabric
- Fusible Interfacing
- Sulky Totally Stable Iron-On Stabilizer
- Sulky 3 mm Puffy Foam - color to
  coordinate with thread color
- Sulky Rayon Embroidery Thread
- Husqvarna Embroidery Library 200900,
  Old English Alphabet
- 1/2" wide Steam-A-Seam 2 Tape
- 4" Bell Pull Hardware -
  available in Craft Stores
- Tassel

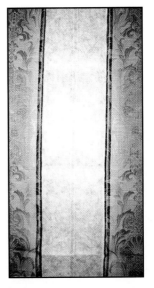

MAKE THE BELL PULL:

1. Cut a 9" x 24" rectangle of striped decorator fabric with the stripe running with the longer side.

2. Serge with a three-thread overlock stitch to clean finish all edges.

3. Cut a 5" x 18" strip of fusible interfacing. Center it on a stripe on the back of the decorator fabric; fuse it on.

4. To determine the placement of the embroidered letters, on the right side starting 5-1/4" down from the top, make a mark with a chalk or air-erasable marker every 2-1/4" along the center, ending 5-1/4" from the bottom.

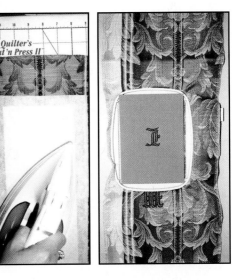

EMBELLISH WITH STITCHING OVER SULKY PUFFY FOAM:

1. To stabilize for embroidery, on the underside, cover the fusible interfacing with Sulky Totally Stable.

2. Cut a piece of Puffy Foam a little larger than the embroidered letter message will be. Spray KK 2000 on it and adhere it to the front center of the fabric.

3. Choose your favorite color(s) of Sulky 40 wt. Rayon Thread and embroider the letters W-E-L-C-O-M-E (from the Husqvarna Embroidery Library 200900, Old English Alphabet) over the Puffy Foam.

4. Tear away the excess Puffy Foam and shrink any fuzzies by holding a steam iron about 1/2" _above_ them and shooting them with steam.

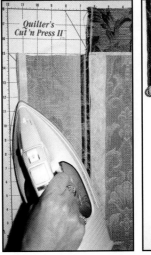

FINISHING:

1. To finish the bell pull, press under each side either _following a stripe as a guide, or so the finished size is 3-3/4" x 18-1/2"._

2. Press 1/2" Steam-A-Seam 2 tape to the wrong side of the overlapping edge. Pull off the paper and press to fuse the overlapping edge to the underneath layer.

3. Fold the top and bottom ends to a point. Trim away excess fabric leaving a 1/4" seam allowance. Insert hardware. Fold the point up and whip-stitch it in place on the back of the bell pull.

A Quick Quilted Project
Rotary Cutter Bag

Designed by Marilyn Fisher

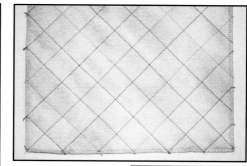

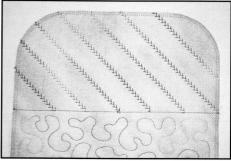

QUILT IT:

1. Attach a darning foot and lower the feed dogs. Free-motion **Stipple Stitch** with a large, meandering stitch throughout the middle section.

2. Use a temporary marker to draw a 45 degree line from top bottom of the lower section. Raise the fe[e] dogs and attach a walking foot and quilting guide.

Set your stitch length at 3.0 to 3.5 and with your quilting guide set at 1", **Crosshatch Stitch** this entire section.

3. In the top 4" section, again using your temporary marker, draw a 45 degree line. Using your walking foot and your quilting guide set at 1", feather stitch diagonal rows across this section.

4. After quilting is complete, serge around the entire piece. Fold up the bottom 8-1/2" section, right sides together and use a 1/4" seam allowance to stitch the sides closed, leaving the top 4" section free.

Note: If you did not serge the edges, you could finish this flap edge with a purchased bias binding to give it a clean look. Also, fold down the top edge 1/4". Do this before sewing the case together so that you catch the binding ends inside the rotary cutter case.

Turn right side out. Mark the center line with a temporary marker and straight stitch this line the entire length of the bag up to the beginning of the flap. Fold 1/4" of the top flap edge toward the inside and topstitch this edge down about 1/8" from the edge. Use Velcro or stitch one piece of 8" to 10" ribbon at the center of the flap and another piece where the flap meets the body of the rotary cutter case. Voila! A quick and easy gift.

SUPPLIES:

- 9" x 21" Cotton fabric for outside of case
- 9" x 21" Cotton fabric for the lining
- 9" x 21" piece of batting
- Sulky 30 wt. #2125 Variegated Rayon Thread
- 14/90 Quilting Needle
- Darning Foot
- Walking Foot with Quilting Guide
- Ruler with a 45-Degree Line
- Temporary Marker
- Velcro or Ribbon for closure
- Optional Purchased bias binding (if you do not use a Serger)
- Sulky KK 2000 Temporary Spray Adhesive

PREPARE FABRIC PIECES:

1. Thread the machine with Sulky 30 wt. Variegated #2125 on the top and in the bobbin. Lay the lining wrong side up and spray it with KK 2000. Place the batting on it. Spray the wrong side of the outside fabric and place it on the batting, right side up.

2. Trim off corners of one end through all three layers to round off. (See photo right.) Divide the quilt sandwich into sections. From top (rounded side) measure down 4", draw a line across with a temporary marker. Stitch across this line. Measure down from this drawn line 8-1/2" and draw another line, leaving another 8-1/2" section below it.

BASIC INSTRUCTIONS FOR SASHINGS, BORDERS, BINDING & BASTING

By Joyce Drexler and Deanna Spingola

Illustrations on pages 157-160 are taken from Deanna's book, **STRIP-PIECED WATERCOLOR MAGIC**
(Used with permission of That Patchwork Place, Bothell, WA)

In this section, you will find photos of various quilts in progress that are included in this book along with descriptions of how to accomplish a certain task in finishing your quilt top. But keep in mind that the procedure would be the same for any quilt top.

ASSEMBLING BLOCKS WITH NO SASHING STRIPS TO CREATE THE QUILT TOP:

1. Lay out the blocks in the order of the "quilt plan" or as the finished quilt photo indicates. Rotate them as necessary to their proper position.

2. Determine which direction to press the vertical seams, then press them to one side. To reduce bulk, press seam allowances in opposite directions from block to block to allow them to nest together.

3. Sew the blocks together in horizontal rows. Press the seams between the blocks in opposite directions from row to row. Sew the rows together. Trim all stray threads from the back.

ADDING SASHING BETWEEN THE BLOCKS TO SEPARATE THE BLOCKS ON THE QUILT TOP:

1. Once the blocks of your quilt are completed, you are ready to add **Sashing Strips** to separate each block from one another. Make sure all blocks are of the same size that are to be in the quilt. Lay out the blocks in the desired order. Cut the Sashing Strips to the same length as the side of the block. Assemble the blocks in horizontal rows. Sew vertical Sashing Strips to both sides of the blocks in each row. Press seams to one side toward the Sashing Strip.

2. Add the horizontal Sashing Strips on each side of the rows. Press the seams to one side toward the Sashing Strip.

CHECK SIZE:

1. Make sure opposite edges of the quilt top are the same length. Fold the quilt in half lengthwise to check the sides, then fold it crosswise to check the top and bottom edges.

2. If opposite edges are unequal, press the seams again to remove any tucks, or take slightly deeper seams on several rows. Make all corrections or adjustments now; any problems will not magically disappear as you continue.

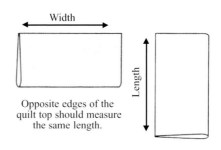

Opposite edges of the quilt top should measure the same length.

CUTTING AND PREPARING *SINGLE BORDERS or BINDING:*

Most of the quilts in this book have simple borders. Some have special continuous line quilting designs and some are plain. We have broken down the procedures for multiple and single bordered quilts as well as mitered corners and square corners. The border should not be so complex that it distracts from the quilt itself; instead, it should give an ending to the blocks like a mat does in a framed photo.

Select the fabrics for the border(s) once the quilt top is finished. Determine which values and colors are most prominent in the quilt top, then audition several fabrics that are compatible with or complement those colors or values. Each quilt plan includes border measurements that correspond to the finished quilt photo. Suggested yardage is given for each quilt project.

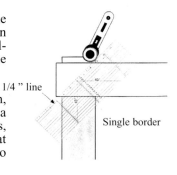

1/4 " line

Single border

All of the quilt border measurements are with the borders cut across the grain, from selvage to selvage. A few have lengthwise borders if the fabric was a border print. When using crosswise strips, piece them by placing two strips, right sides together, at a 90° angle. Position the 1/4" line of a ruler exactly at the intersection of the two strips and trim as shown. Pin, then sew the two pieces together, using a 1/4" wide seam allowance. Press the seam open.

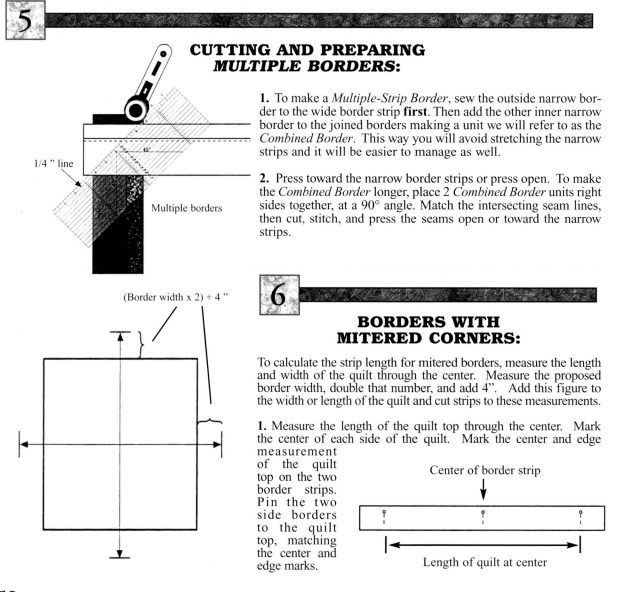

CUTTING AND PREPARING *MULTIPLE BORDERS:*

1/4 " line

Multiple borders

1. To make a *Multiple-Strip Border*, sew the outside narrow border to the wide border strip **first**. Then add the other inner narrow border to the joined borders making a unit we will refer to as the *Combined Border*. This way you will avoid stretching the narrow strips and it will be easier to manage as well.

2. Press toward the narrow border strips or press open. To make the *Combined Border* longer, place 2 *Combined Border* units right sides together, at a 90° angle. Match the intersecting seam lines, then cut, stitch, and press the seams open or toward the narrow strips.

(Border width x 2) + 4 "

BORDERS WITH MITERED CORNERS:

To calculate the strip length for mitered borders, measure the length and width of the quilt through the center. Measure the proposed border width, double that number, and add 4". Add this figure to the width or length of the quilt and cut strips to these measurements.

1. Measure the length of the quilt top through the center. Mark the center of each side of the quilt. Mark the center and edge measurement of the quilt top on the two border strips. Pin the two side borders to the quilt top, matching the center and edge marks.

Center of border strip

Length of quilt at center

2. Mark the quilt corners 1/4" in from corner points. Pin the border strips to the quilt top with right sides together up to the 1/4" marks. Stitch with the border on the bottom and the quilt top wrong side up so you can guide the block seams in the proper direction. Start and stop the stitching 1/4" from each edge. Press the seam allowances toward the border.

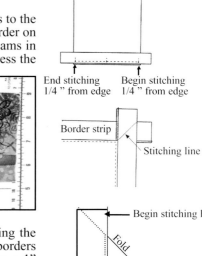

End stitching 1/4" from edge   Begin stitching 1/4" from edge

Border strip   Stitching line

3. Measure the width of the quilt top through the center. Do not include the side borders. Mark, pin, and stitch the top and bottom border strips to the quilt as you did the side borders. Press the seam allowance toward the borders.

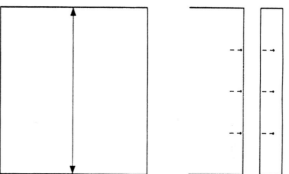

4. To miter the first corner, place the quilt wrong side up on a flat, hard ironing surface. Overlap the two border strips at a 90° angle. Fold to the back in a perfect 45° angle using the ruler markings to check the angle. Extensions should line up. Narrow borders should match perfectly. Spray lightly with sizing and press lightly. Iron a 1" wide strip of Sulky Totally Stable over the miter on the right side. Turn the quilt top over in a handkerchief fold. Crease. Stitch on the crease. Press mitered borders open and trim to 1/4". Repeat for remaining corners.

Begin stitching here

Fold

Border   Wrong side of quilt

7

BORDERS WITH STRAIGHT-CUT CORNERS:

Note: If you are adding more than one border with straight-cut corners to your quilt, add each one separately. Measure as suggested below after each opposing pair of borders is added. DO NOT SEW THEM TOGETHER BEFORE ATTACHING THEM.

1. To calculate the strip length for straight-cut borders, measure the length of the quilt through the center. Cut two side borders to that length. Fold the two border strips in half, then in quarters. With a pin, mark each division. Repeat with the quilt top to mark the same divisions. Pin the border strips to the quilt, matching the markings.

2. Stitch the border strips to the quilt top, easing as necessary. Stitch with the quilt top on top so you can guide the quilt top seams in the proper direction. Press the seam allowances toward the border.

3. Measure the width of the quilt top through the center, including the side borders. Cut the top and bottom border strips to that length. Fold and mark the edge of the quilt and border strips as before. Pin the strips to the quilt, matching the markings.

4. Stitch the border strips to the top and bottom of the quilt top, easing as necessary. Press the seam allowances toward the border.

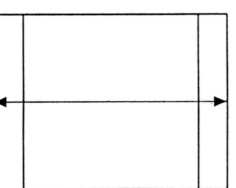

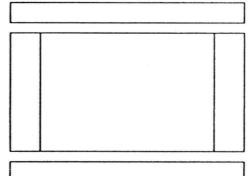

8

PREPARE TO QUILT:

1. Choose a batting such as Fairfield Low-Loft for machine quilting. Take it out of the package and lay it flat overnight. If you choose cotton batting, you may wish to pre-shrink it.

2. Piece together the backing fabric so that it extends 3-4" beyond the quilt top all the way around the quilt. Secure it, right side down, to a hard surface with Painter's Masking Tape or Bull Clips (if using a table).

3. Lay the batting over the backing and fold it over on itself lengthwise. Lightly spray KK 2000 Temporary Spray Adhesive on the exposed half of the backing fabric. Hold the can 6-10" away from the surface you are spraying. Unfold and smooth out the batting over the sprayed area. Fold over the other half of the batting and spray the backing fabric. Unfold and smooth out the batting.

4. Lay the quilt top right side up over the batting. Fold it over on itself lengthwise, lightly spray the wrong side with KK-2000, and smooth out the sprayed side over the batting. Fold back the other side, lightly spray it with KK 2000, and smooth it out over the batting. Spraying with KK 2000 will greatly reduce the need for pin basting and it will hold the quilt sandwich together while quilting without staining the fabric.

Horizontal seam

Vertical seam

One full and two half-widths of backing fabric

9

PREPARING A *HANGING SLEEVE:*

1. Trim the outside edge of the quilt so all layers are even. Use a Quilter's Ruler and measure out from the last border seam to achieve an equal measurement all around.

2. Cut and piece, if necessary, a 4-1/2" wide strip the width of the quilt. Fold in the short ends 1 inch making a smooth edge. Fold wrong sides together lengthwise. Press. Place the Hanging Sleeve on the back of the quilt so the raw edges of the top of the quilt and the raw edges of the sleeve match. Pin. Sew a scant 1/4" seam.

Right side of sleeve

Wrong side of quilt

10

CUTTING AND PREPARING *BINDING:*

1. Cut 2-1/4" to 2-1/2" x 44" strips. Use the same technique to join binding strips as described in #4 on page 158 making one continuous strip long enough to go all the way around the raw edge of the quilt.

2. Fold wrong sides together lengthwise so raw edges of the binding strip meet. Press along fold.

3. Lay the Binding Strip so folded edge faces into the quilt top. Match the raw edges to the raw edges of the right side of the quilt. Pin in place. Refer to #6 and #7 on page 159 and handle the corners in the same elected method you have chosen for the Borders. Sew using a 1/4" to 3/8" seam.

4. Fold the Binding over the raw edge of the quilt. Pin or clip to hold in place. Hand Whip Stitch the folded edge to the back of the quilt making sure stitches don't show on front of the quilt.

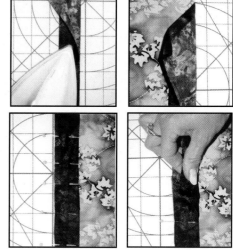

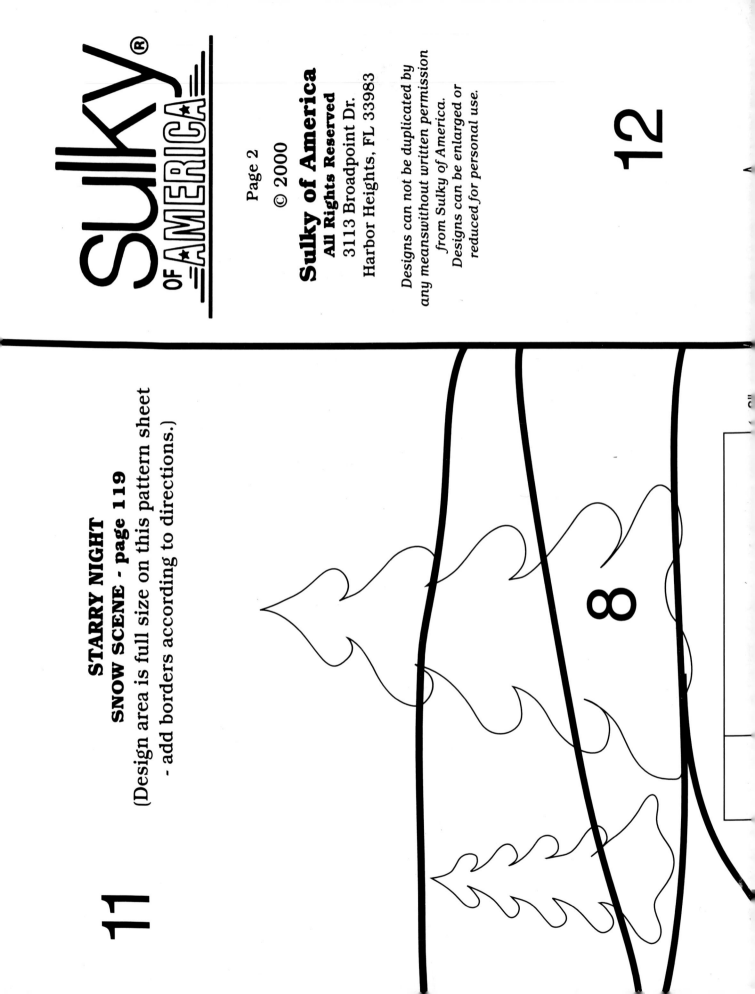

12

STARRY NIGHT
SNOW SCENE - page 119
(Design area is full size on this pattern sheet - add borders according to directions.)

8

11

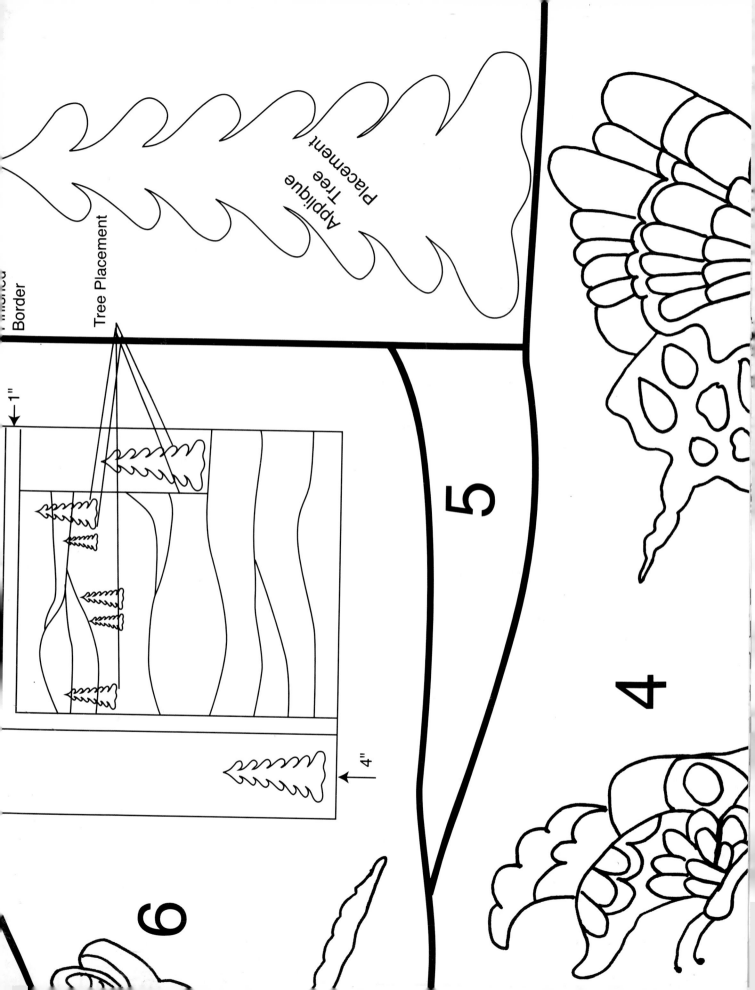